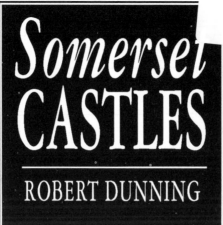

Somerset CASTLES

ROBERT DUNNING

Somerset Books

First published in 1995 by Somerset Books

ISBN 1 861832 78 7

British Library Cataloguing-in-Publication Data
CIP data for this book is available from the British Library

SOMERSET BOOKS
Official publisher to
Somerset County Council
Halsgrove House
Lower Moor Way
Tiverton EX16 6SS

Telephone: 01884 243242
Facsimile: 01884 243325

Printed and bound in Great Britain
by Longdunn Press Ltd, Bristol

Front cover illustration: Taunton Castle by L.C. Hammett.
Back cover photograph: Bridgwater Castle (from the seal of the
Corporation of Bridgwater).

SOMERSET CASTLES

ACKNOWLEDGEMENTS

The author acknowledges with many thanks the help of Bob Croft and Chris Webster who read and commented most helpfully on the text; of Joan Hasler, John Post and Hugh Prudden who provided particular pieces of information and prints with exemplary speed; of Mick Aston, who has been most generous in his permission to use his work among the illustrations; and of the Somerset Archaeological and Natural History Society, whose superb collection of illustrative material has again proved a rich quarry. Tom Mayberry, Honorary Editor of the Society's *Proceedings*, has given permission on behalf of the Society for the use of illustrations appearing among its papers insofar as copyright lies with the Society. Illustrations from the collections of the British Library are reproduced by permission of British Library Reproductions.

Acknowledgements of and sources for illustrations on the following pages are:

Mick Aston – 27b, 34, 69, 74a; author – 20b, 25, 35, 38, 44, 47, 56b, 59, 63, 77; Blake Museum, Bridgwater – 29; British Library – 14a (Add. MS. 33717, f. 171, J. Skinner), 19 (Add. MS. 18674, f. 28,? H. Wigstead), 67 (Egerton MS 3102, f. 201, J. Skinner); Devon County Council – 10; Jeremy Dunning – back cover; the late Peter Greening – 6; Jim Hancock – 36, 58; Hugh Prudden – 42a; Somerset Archaeological and Natural History Society – front cover (watercolour by Miss L.C. Hammett 1921), 17 (J. Buckler), 21 (W. Watts), 26 (W.W. Wheatley), 39b (J. Buckler), 46b (S. & N. Buck), 49, 51, 54a (J. Buckler), 54b, 56a (W.W. Wheatley), 68 (J. Buckler), 70 (A.A. Clarke), 73 (W.W. Wheatley), 78a, 78b (S. & H. Grimm); Somerset Archaeological and Natural History Society, *Proceedings* – 7, 9, 14b (I. Burrow), 18 (J.H.P. Gibb), 23 (M. Batt), 27a (D.Hill), 28 (C. Sidaway), 39a (J.H.P. Gibb), 57 (R. Wilcox); Somerset County Council, Department for the Environment – 6 (after P. Webb), 7, 12, 16, 27b, 43, 52; Somerset County Council, Local History Library – 72 (Iris Hardwick), 74b, 76 (?Robert Gillo); the late W.J. Wedlake, 53.

SOMERSET CASTLES

Introduction

The definition of the word castle for the purposes of this book goes beyond the usual one of a building which was both a military fortress and the residence of a feudal lord. That is not to deny the accepted wisdom that castle building was introduced with feudalism from Normandy with the Conquest, but simply to enable the *burhs* which formed an important line of defence across the south of England in the early tenth century to be seen as the 'communal' castles they were, providing safe haven in the face of Danish invasions.

The definition is drawn even wider for, while rejecting prehistoric earthworks later named castles which bear no evidence of pre- or post-Conquest military use, it embraces the fortified manor house where the chief feature is either a gatehouse or a moat, even in the absence of a strong surrounding wall with some evidence of wall-walks and sheltering parapet. To complete the story, the definition also includes follies built from the early seventeenth century onwards which attempted in some way to recreate a castle ruin, and also three houses whose names and form were a conscious re-creation of a medieval military past.

The Burghal Hidage, c. 914

Danish attacks around the English coast were countered, probably from the late ninth century, the reign of Alfred (871-899), by the creation of a chain of strongholds constructed of earth and timber and designed for communal defence. A document known as the Burghal Hidage, probably drawn up about 914 by Edward the Elder, Alfred's son, is a list of such strongholds or *burhs* spread across most of southern England. Five are in Somerset: Watchet, Lyng, Langport, Axbridge and Bath. The *burh* at Watchet, now known as Daw's Castle, occupies a commanding position on the cliffs between Watchet and Old Cleeve overlooking a stretch of coastline often plundered by the Danes. Lyng secured the marshes near the royal monastic foundation of Athelney; Langport controlled the upper reaches of the Parrett and the entrance to the royal estate of Somerton; Axbridge stood at the narrow part of the Axe valley covering access to the royal palace at Cheddar; and Bath, with its substantially surviving Roman walls, was the entrance to the Cotswolds and the way the Saxon invaders had themselves come centuries before from the Thames valley. It is curious that South Cadbury played no formal role in this scheme, though it was certainly occupied in the Late Saxon period.

A number of hides (a measure of land) was assigned to each *burh* in the Burghal Hidage to produce an adequate number of men for its defence. Contemporary wisdom required 16 hides for the maintenance and defence of an acre's breadth of

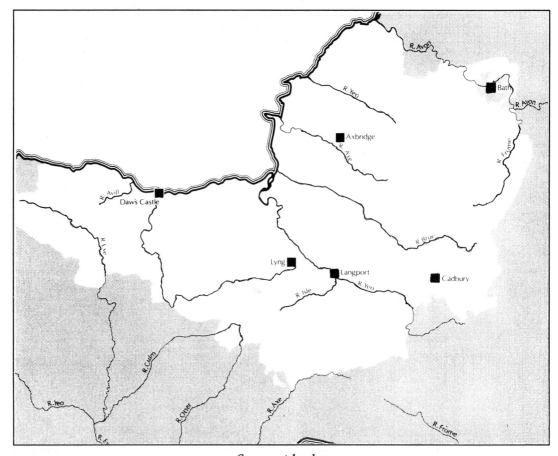

Somerset burhs

wall and thus four men to defend a furlong. Watchet's 513 hides implied a bank or wall of over 700 yards; Lyng's 100 hides suggest a length of just over 412 feet, Langport 825 yards, Axbridge 550 yards, Bath 1375 yards. Fieldwork at Lyng and Axbridge has produced suggestions for the location of the defences based on these arrangements, and maps and excavation at Bath have established a close correlation between the tenth-century calculation and the Roman and later medieval city wall.

The castles of the Norman Conquest

Communal defence in the tenth century gave place to the military strongholds represented by the motte-and-bailey castles introduced by the Normans immediately after 1066. The new lords had to make their power felt quickly and essentially their castles comprised man-made or natural mounds (*mottes*) surmounted by timber structures, each connected to a yard or bailey surrounded by bank and ditch, the bank probably topped with a timber wall.

Daw's Castle, Watchet

William the Conqueror himself had no castles in Somerset in 1066, but his loyal followers Walter or Walschin of Douai and William de Mohun were given estates in strategic parts of the county, several of them indicating that the sons of the defeated King Harold, himself formerly earl of Wessex, continued to be a threat along the coast. The county was obviously vulnerable to sea-borne attack and the castles which may be ascribed to Walter of Douai and William de Mohun at Worle and Dunster, and possibly the fortresses at Over Stowey, perhaps the work of Alfred d'Epaignes (or of Spain), and at Locking seem to follow the same purpose as the *burhs* of Alfred and Edward the Elder, namely a first line of defence against sea-borne invasion.

Walter of Douai or his son Robert may have built at least three other castles further

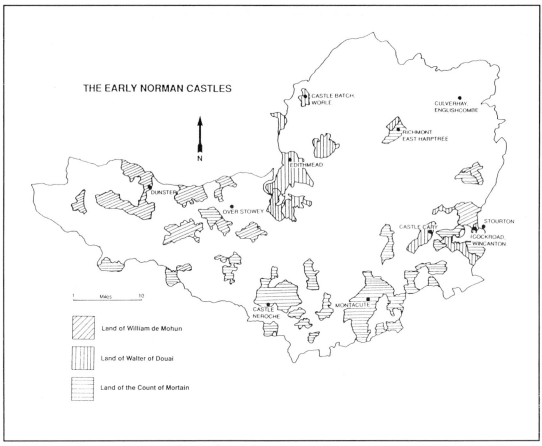

The castles of the Norman Conquest

inland, but still of strategic significance. In 1086 Walter held West Harptree manor controlling a route across the Mendips and other manors at Cary and Wincanton where the approaches into Selwood Forest might be defended. His son Robert of Bampton, also called Robert son of Walter, was the count of Mortain's tenant at East Harptree. It seems beyond simple coincidence that there were motte-and-bailey castles at East Harptree, Cary and Wincanton, as well as another just over the Wiltshire border but still in Selwood at Stourton (also held by Walter of Douai), and yet another just over the Devon border at Bampton, Robert's principal fortress.

In addition Robert, count of Mortain and half-brother of the Conqueror, built one, and possibly two, in the south of the county, not to guard against coastal invasion from the north but to be ready for possible insurrection by native English. Domesday Book, compiled in 1086, records that on one of his Somerset manors (he held 797 manors, most of them in Cornwall) was his castle of Montacute, on a manor then called Bishopston. Almost immediately after the Conquest he had acquired Bishopston from Athelney abbey in order to take advantage of the steep natural hill above the village. It very soon become the motte of a fortress suitable for such a mighty baron. It was perhaps the first Norman castle in the county for in 1068 it was besieged by an army of English rebels. The need for these castles of conquest was thus proved.

By 1086 many of the count's estates were held of him by tenants, but he retained in his own control two manors in particular, Bishopston and Staple, each in the centre of a compact block of his land. For almost twenty years a formidable castle served as a statement of feudal power at Montacute, the centre of one group of holdings. It seems likely that the same count built a second castle at the centre of his other block of land, a castle later known as Castle Neroche.

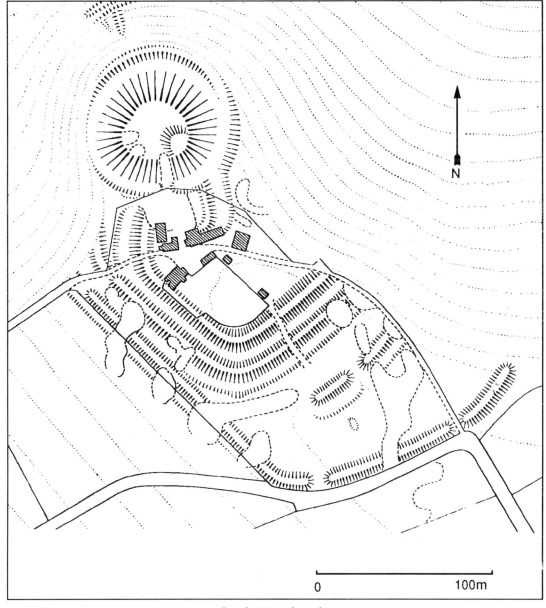

Castle Neroche: plan

Most of the count's Somerset land was held of him by his own leading supporters, men who had come with him from the neighbourhood of Mortain in Normandy and who were part of his baronial household: Alfred the Butler, Drogo or Drew of Montacute, Robert the Constable, Ansger Brito, Mauger of Cartrai and Bretel of St Clair. The small manor of Steart in Babcary was held by two unnamed men who were described as porters of Montacute. Alfred, Drogo and Bretel held estates widely spread in the county but also two important little pieces of land in Bishopston manor; they could be on hand whenever the count kept court at Montacute.

In 1088, only two years after Domesday Book was compiled, the count of Mortain was involved in a rebellion against William Rufus and in favour of the king's brother Robert. He died at the end of 1090. His son and successor, William, took part in Robert of Belleme's rebellion in Normandy against Henry I and after defeat at Tinchebrai in April 1106 the great Mortain holding in England was taken from the count and was divided into a number of smaller baronies. The heart of the Somerset fief, Montacute, became the endowment of a Cluniac monastery at the end of the street still known as Bishopston and the castle immediately lost both its administrative and its military significance. The fortress at Staple was also evidently abandoned, though possibly it later came to have a function in the royal forest of Neroche which developed around and east of it during the next century.

Dunster

The larger tenants of the disgraced count of Mortain remained undisturbed and their holdings themselves came to be called baronies held directly from the Crown, their size and importance calculated by the number of knights' fees each was worth. At least some of the manors held in 1086 by Alfred the Butler including Chinnock, Pendomer, Chilthorne and Chiselborough, became the barony of Chiselborough. Odcombe, Lufton, Houndstone and Trent became the Brito barony of Odcombe; Bretel of St Clair and his descendants held the barony of Stoke Trister; Robert the Constable the barony of Hatch; Drogo of Montacute's family owned estates whose centre was Shepton Montague.

No castles are known to have been built on these baronies since the need for military strongholds had passed. Yet baronies and fees continued to be recorded for the purposes of feudal taxation. In 1166 Richard FitzWilliam, grandson of Alfred the Butler, held ten knights' fees, described as fees of Mortain, in Somerset and Dorset; his tenants included William of Chinnock (one fee), Ralph of Domer (two fees at Pen) and William of Chilthorne (one fee). In the same year Walter Brito, descendant of Ansger, held 15 fees including Odcombe. Presumably the lords of these fees built homes for themselves and their families, but none has yet been identified as surviving from that time although the former manor houses at Hatch Beauchamp and Yarlington may well have occupied ancient sites and the manor house at Stoke Trister may still do so.

William de Mohun, the Conqueror's third loyal supporter in the county, was the builder of Dunster castle, one of the two (Montacute was the other) recorded in Somerset in Domesday Book. Like its contemporaries it was at first of the motte-and-bailey type, a conical hill made more formidable by scarping with an adjoining area defended with a bank and ditch, in this case made particularly formidable by its position on a natural rocky cliff above an inlet of the sea.

From castles of conquest to feudal strongholds

Within a century of the Conquest other feudal estates had developed from the holdings of the principal Domesday landlords. They were owned by men who were rich and influential enough to build castles which, in the context of the times, had more of political than of military significance. Tenants and neighbours were to be impressed rather than dominated. Thus in 1166 Philip de Columbers, successor of the Domesday tenant Alfred d'Epaignes, had a stronghold at Nether Stowey. It stood at the head (*caput*) of the 'honor' or barony of Nether Stowey which was reckoned by the king's exchequer to produce ten knights when required. Those ten knights were Columbers tenants, most of them holding land not far from the castle; men prepared to come in person when the castle needed defence or repair, or to pay a cash equivalent. Plud Farmhouse in Kilton parish was for long remembered as the residence of the castle constable [1].

Nether Stowey

The castle of Nether Stowey itself was still the traditional motte-and-bailey type, the motte sited on a natural hill with a good view of the coast, better than that enjoyed by Alfred d'Epaignes's fortress at Over Stowey. The building on the motte was, however, probably from the first in stone; it was no emergency structure but a castle whose creator had had time to plan and build at leisure.

In 1166, when Philip de Columbers was owner of the barony of Nether Stowey, William de Curci was in possession of the barony of Stogursey. The barony was larger than Nether Stowey, reckoned to produce 27 knights, but little is known of the castle at the time beyond some twelfth-century stonework in the surviving curtain wall. Most of the information to survive about Croft castle, in Crewkerne parish, is that it was maintained and probably garrisoned in the early twelfth century by the neighbouring tenants of Richard and Baldwin de Redvers, earls of Devon. It was thus the focal point of the family's estates concentrated in south Somerset and north Dorset.

The records of the owners of Dunster show that by the mid twelfth century the castle had been transformed from its original role as a castle of conquest to the centre of the extensive barony of the Mohun family. It suffered more than one attack in its long history, but it was as the administrative and political centre of a great estate that its real importance is seen. Until the early thirteenth century the duty of castle maintenance was expected of certain knights and free tenants who held land of the 'honor' of Dunster, but Reginald Mohun (died 1258) released several of these military tenants from their obligation to repair and strengthen the upper ward in return for cash to build the lower ward[2].

A century earlier, in 1138, the castle was already an impressive structure, having towers and walls which must have been of stone. William de Mohun, then the owner, 'collected bands of horsemen and footmen', and terrorised the surrounding countryside. The strength of the castle and its position were such that King Stephen did not attempt a frontal attack but his troops under Henry de Tracy 'made vigorous and determined attacks' and captured over a hundred of Mohun's horsemen. The record of these events does not say that the castle was ever taken, only that William was humiliated[3]. In the early thirteenth century the castle defences were strengthened by order of the king when the castle was in King John's hands during the minority of the heir [4].

Castles of revolt

Periods of political uncertainty in any part of the country would heighten the importance of local castles and it was said that in 1153, at the end of the civil war between Stephen and Matilda, 1115 'adulterine', that is unlicensed, castles were destroyed[5]. Dunster, Cary and Richmont at East Harptree were among castles whose owners were directly involved in the struggle against Stephen, and the king's supporter Henry de Tracy, who managed to defeat William de Mohun at Dunster, also constructed some kind of siege fortress at Cary. It is possible that the earthwork known as Bury castle was an unlicensed stronghold, since William de Say, who probably owned it at his death in 1144, was closely related to Geoffrey de Mandeville, earl of Essex, one of the leading figures in the struggle.

On the king's side was Robert, bishop of Bath, whose see city was attacked by the men of Bristol. Its defences were strengthened by the king's order in 1138. The last phase of Castle Neroche may perhaps be associated with the same period of civil disturbance during Stephen's reign.

Castles in towns

Most of the county's castles stand on sites chosen because natural advantages were combined with ownership by someone of political power and influence. Two, however, Taunton and Bridgwater, share with William the Conqueror's great Tower of London sites integrated into towns. In certain circumstances they could be

Richmont, East Harptree

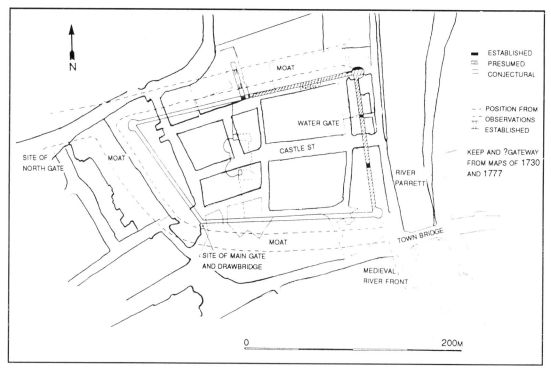

Bridgwater: plan

14

defended, but their military importance was usually secondary to their value as administrative or political centres.

The castle at Taunton was first mentioned in 1138 among a list of properties of Henry of Blois, bishop of Winchester and the influential half-brother of King Stephen. By that date it included a large, rectangular tower keep. How much such a building was the product of personal whim and how much practical necessity may be gauged by the fact that Bishop Henry had similar castles on several of his other Winchester bishopric estates.

Bridgwater, which occupied one quarter of the fortified town, came into being at the same time as the town in the sense that both were built under royal licences issued in 1200. It is just possible that the natural strength of the site on rising ground beside the Parrett may have been defended earlier, although there is no surviving written evidence to support the idea.

Castles in use

Castles came into prominence at times of political unrest. The uncertainties raised by the policies of King John in the early thirteenth century may well have been the cause of the royal order to strengthen Dunster, then under the control of the king's over-loyal servant Hubert de Burgh. The political situation may also have been the reason why another of John's henchmen, William Brewer, was licensed to build at Bridgwater; and why John's Justiciar, Peter des Roches, improved the defences both of his castle and town at Taunton.

The colourful political careers of Stogursey's owners in the early years of Henry III's reign found the castle at first under threat of destruction, then besieged, then surrendered and finally strengthened. In the 1260s, when Simon de Montfort was opposing the Crown, Taunton was prepared for war and later served as a prison for one of de Montfort's sons.

Other castles still in use in the thirteenth century were presumably owned by men who had no political interests. Those which had never progressed beyond a motte-and-bailey with simple timber superstructure had generally been abandoned, for they could hardly have been held against sophisticated and powerful means of attack. The recorded visit of the lady of Croft castle in 1267-8 was probably her last. By the early fourteenth century there were only four castles in the county of much significance: Bridgwater, Taunton, Dunster, and Stogursey. Bridgwater was for a time of some strategic importance when it was taken by the Crown in the 1320s as a base for military operations in Wales and as part of the political struggle with the Mortimers, though the size of its garrison – four men-at-arms and 18 cross-bow men and archers – seems less than impressive. The other three had become the headquarters of increasingly sophisticated estates.

Designed to impress: castle or fortified house?

The forts of the Burghal Hidage and the motte-and-bailey structures of the eleventh century were essentially military in concept; they were for the defence of the realm against possible Danish attack in the tenth century and for the defence of strategic estates as the Norman aristocrats established themselves and their regime in the countryside. Defence of a regime in a more formal feudal sense remained a principal purpose in the twelfth century. At the same time there was room for the personal expression of a grandiose whim, such as the so-called castle Henry of Blois built to serve as his residence within the monastic precinct at Glastonbury.

There were other landlords whose means would not allow them to aspire to a proper castle but whose tastes were still for the grand on a minor scale. 'Moats as a gesture to security' or 'crenellation as a decorative motif and as a gesture to tradition and prestige'[6] were not a sign that the castle was in decline, simply that there were landowners with slender purses. And to moats and crenellations might reasonably be added towers or gatehouses.

Thus at the end of the twelfth century there was a *castellarium* at Brent Marsh, the work of a prosperous Glastonbury abbey tenant. By the end of the thirteenth century there may well have been a moat at Marsh Court in Wincanton (there was a

Marston Moat, Marston Bigot

chapel there in 1280) and fortified towers or gatehouses at East Quantoxhead and Clevedon.

In the fourteenth century the spread of crenellated houses can be charted by reference to the issue of royal licences to the new men of influence in the county: in 1313 to Simon de Montacute for Yarlington, in 1316 to Adam Brett at the instance of the king's nurse for Torweston, and in 1333 to John de Beauchamp for Hatch and Stoke sub Hamdon. Marston is known to have been licensed by Edward II, and Newton St Loe belongs to the early fourteenth century on architectural grounds. The bishop's palace at Wells was walled and moated in 1340 in the face of local political unrest; and Merryfield, West Bower and probably Norton sub Hamdon were also fortified in the fourteenth century.

Two other buildings, erected towards the end of the fourteenth century, demonstrate perfectly that castles are objects of conspicuous spending. Nunney, licensed in 1373, seems to be the work of a man who wanted to show his neighbours how well he had done from his military service in France. It bore, of course, all the traits of a military fortification, but its site was hardly suitable for adequate defence and Sir John de la Mare had no feudal and very little political power. Sir Thomas Hungerford, in contrast, was a powerful man in Parliament and influential enough to obtain a royal pardon in 1383 for fortifying his house at Farleigh without licence. Its site, on a hill, could have been chosen for military reasons, but like Nunney it was little more than

Nash 'Priory', East Coker: gatehouse, 1837

a fortified courtyard house. Nash and West Bower illustrate another feature of the courtyard house, for in both the gatehouse seems to have been the principal building. This, too, was a matter of social status, but the survival of many less impressive gatehouses throughout the county (e.g. Whatley, Chew Magna, Combe Sydenham, Cothay) and written references to others (e.g. Enmore and Plainsfield)[7] are evidence that owners of small houses as much as owners of castles built to impress.

Decline, revival and destruction

John Leland, visiting Somerset in the 1540s, noted that Richmont and Stoke were in ruins, Bridgwater was becoming ruinous and Dunster, Farleigh, Nunney, and Wells were still in use. From other sources it is known that Stogursey had then recently been restored for use as estate headquarters and Taunton had been partly rebuilt and extended, essentially for the same purpose.

Dunster: Sir Hugh Luttrell's gatehouse

Significant building had been undertaken at Taunton, Stogursey, Farleigh, and especially at Dunster during the course of the fifteenth century. It was surely right and proper that Sir Hugh Luttrell, the first of his line to occupy Dunster, should have altered his new home in a military style in keeping both with the times and with his distinguished career in the service of John of Gaunt, Richard II, Henry IV and Henry V. He was evidently not at Agincourt in 1415 but in the following year he was serving in Harfleur and in 1417 he undertook to raise 80 men for the army. Later he was to serve as lieutenant of Harfleur and seneschal of Normandy, positions of considerable trust in the newly-won territory.

From almost the first year of his possession of the castle, Sir Hugh spent money on repairs and maintenance, but in 1417 he paid the expenses of a Bridgwater mason who came 'to see my lord's hall in the Castle which is to be rebuilt'. Between 1420 and 1424 the hall was evidently altered and a great gatehouse built, the whole works costing a total of over £250. The result was a statement of power and possession[8].

The same motive probably inspired Sir Walter Hungerford, like Luttrell a veteran of the French wars, whose building of a second ward at Farleigh in the 1440s involved not only the construction of a new gateway, curtain walls and towers but evidently the removal of nearby houses and the building of a new parish church to replace the original which had now become the castle chapel. Such conspicuous extravagance was perhaps to be expected from a man who had been promoted to the ranks of the baronage and saw himself as one of the new political lords of the West Country, able and willing to impress friend and foe alike.

Farleigh Hungerford, c. 1746

It is significant that one of the new rooms fitted out at Stogursey by the earl of Northumberland from the 1490s was an audit room, and that work at Taunton during the same period should have included alterations to the gatehouse which served as the exchequer for the Winchester bishopric estates in the neighbourhood.

New families in the county, rising by judicious marriages and persisting by the good fortune of healthy heirs or political acumen, often preferred to impress with a more comfortable magnificence. Clevedon Court or Stoke sub Hamdon in the fourteenth and Cothay and Fairfield in the fifteenth centuries were sufficiently impressive for their domestic purpose but still retained, by towers or curtain walls, some notion of their military origins, for their founders were knights, in landed wealth if not by strict title, and a knight must, almost by definition, live in a castle. And this was a notion which persisted in Montacute House, the county's outstanding example of Renaissance building. The formal walled garden on the east side of the house, with its delicate pavilions and gatehouse leading to the park, is surely an echo of the castle courtyard through which the visitor, suitably impressed by its magnificence, entered the great hall.

An Indian summer

None of the battles of the Wars of the Roses took place in Somerset, but Taunton castle was involved shortly before the outbreak of more general fighting when in August 1451 the earl of Devon marched with a considerable force from the town against the earl of Wiltshire and then returned to find Lord Bonville in occupation. Devon laid siege to the castle for three days but was persuaded to withdraw by the duke of York. Bonville handed over the castle to York[9].

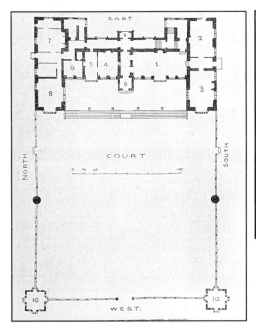

Left: Montacute House: plan
Above: Montacute House: pavilion

Five castles were returned to their original military purpose during the Civil War of the seventeenth century and Dunster's natural strength ensured that it was the last to be surrendered. The successful defence of Taunton had perhaps more to do with the personal determination of its defenders than the strength of its walls. Bridgwater was certainly in no state to be held, and Nunney's site proved how vulnerable it was against cannon. Nevertheless the potential nuisance value of the county's castles, however ruinous, persuaded the Commonwealth government that slighting or demolition were preferable. The works around Bath were to be slighted in 1646, and so were some new works at Bridgwater. There was some demolition at Dunster in 1651 and the owner was required to promise not to allow any enemy to use it. Probably Taunton suffered most: its great keep was pulled down and outside walls were rendered indefensible[10].

For half a century before the war Dunster had in reality become a country house although its medieval walls and gatehouse had been so formidable an obstacle to besiegers. By the end of the century Bridgwater had largely given way to a mansion and Taunton was to follow. Elsewhere, the very ruins took on the air not of decline but of romance. Capability Brown's plan of the 1760s for Joseph Langton's park at Newton included drives which allowed guests to admire the ruins of the castle of the St Loes as their carriages conveyed them around his two great lakes. In the 1820s Bishop George Henry Law's 'good taste and judgement' allowed him to pull

Enmore, 1783

down the south wall of the medieval great hall of the Palace at Wells to form a 'picturesque object' in his flower garden. And where there was no castle to dismantle, it was perfectly possible to build a ruin.

There were those, perhaps again wanting to impress, who chose rather to recreate the medieval castle in a different idiom: Enmore in conscious antiquarianism, Midford and Compton Pauncefoot in splendidly imaginative appreciation of the eccentricity of the feudal dwelling whose story covers, in Somerset as elsewhere, a thousand years of history.

REFERENCES

1. *V.C.H. Somerset*, v. 194-5.
2. *Honour of Dunster*, ed. H.C. Maxwell-Lyte (Somerset Record Society, xxxiii), lvi.
3. H. C. Maxwell-Lyte, *History of Dunster*, 6, 350.
4. *Honour of Dunster*, lv.
5. R. Allen Brown, *English Castles*, 82 (quoting Robert of Torigni).
6. Brown, *English Castles*, 128.
7. *V.C.H. Somerset*, vi. 39, 163.
8. Maxwell-Lyte, *History of Dunster*, 80-105.
9. R. A. Griffiths, *The Reign of Henry VI* (1981), 576.
10. M. W. Thompson, *The Decline of the Castle*, 179-85.

GAZETTEER

Inclusion in this gazetteer is not an indication that the castles, houses or sites are accessible to the public. Many of the earthworks are Scheduled Ancient Monuments.

BURHS

AXBRIDGE   ST432545

The name means 'burh by the Axe' and a roughly rectangular area with a boundary approximating to the 550 yards implied by the 400 hides recorded in the Burghal Hidage has been identified to the south of the later medieval and present market place. Although not particularly close to the river, it would nevertheless serve as a base for a force defending the narrow part of the Axe valley against potential attack on the royal palace at Cheddar. (*Proc. Som. Arch. Soc.* cxix. 22-5)

BATH

The actual length of Bath's Roman and medieval walls was 1250 yards, a reasonably close approximation to the 1375 yards calculated from the 1000 hides recorded in the Burghal Hidage. By this time the town was sufficiently important to have the death of its headman or reeve recorded in the Anglo-Saxon Chronicle.

Axbridge: location of burh

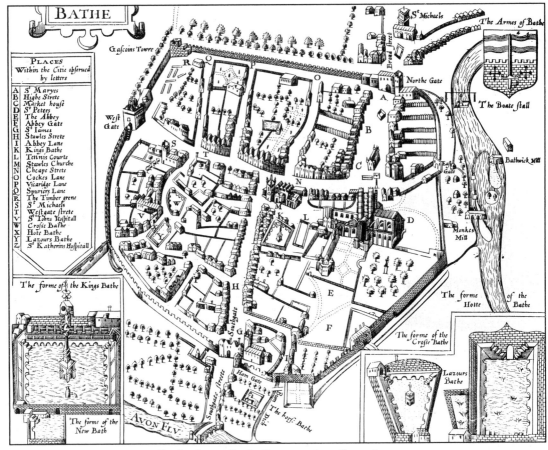

Legend on map:

BATHE

PLACES
Within the Citie obserued
by letters

A S.t Maryes
B Highe Strete
C Market house
D S.t Peters
E The Abbey
F Abbey Gate
G S.t Iames
H Stawles Strete
I Abbey Lane
K Kings Bathe
L Tennis Courte
M Stawles Churche
N Cheape Strete
O Cockes Lane
P Vicaridge Lane
Q Spuriers Lane
R The Timber grene
S S.t Michaels
T Westgate strete
V S.t Iohns Hospitall
W Crosse Bathe
X Hote Bathe
Y Lazours Bathe
Z S.t Katherins Hospitall

Bath: the walls in the seventeenth century

The walls were to be heightened and outworks constructed by order of King Stephen in 1138 after an attack by the men of Bristol. (*Proc. Som. Arch. Soc.* cx. 92)

CADBURY CASTLE,   ST628252
South Cadbury

'Sumtyme a famose toun or castelle', wrote Leland in 1542, and archaeologists in the 1960s demonstrated how the Iron-Age hillfort had actually begun life as a settlement site in the Neolithic period; and again, after desertion, as the site of a hamlet in the Late Bronze Age, and a defended village in the Early Iron Age. Leland's famous town might be recognised in the later years of the Iron Age up to the time of the destruction of its defences and the removal of its inhabitants by an attacking Roman force about AD 70. Then it was a place with strong and sophisticated military defences, a place of craftsmanship and commerce.

The tradition of Cadbury current in Leland's time (just possibly then of fairly recent creation) called it the Camelot of Arthur. The idea came to have some reality in the 1960s when it was found that new defences had been built on a grand scale about the year

South Cadbury

AD 470. These defences included a gate tower, and construction was on a scale only possible with a large labour force for a large garrison. Within these defences was a huge timber hall and among the artefacts found were quantities of pottery indicating a wealthy community with taste for the good things of the Mediterranean world. Was this, asked the archaeologists, the forward base for the defence of the south-west against the advancing Saxons in the campaign culminating in the 'Arthurian' victory at Badon in 490 or 499?

After this date for perhaps five hundred years the old fortress was again abandoned, but its natural strength was recognised in the reign of Ethelred II when either in 1009 or 1010 it became an additional fortress in the defence of Wessex against the Vikings.

Known as the *burh* of Cadanbyrig, it had a commercial and administrative as well as a military role. It was a place secure enough to establish a mint, in this case one removed from the more vulnerable Ilchester. But the new town did not last for long; moneyers only worked there until 1019 and the slight foundations of a church found there is clear evidence of a building only just begun. The whole hilltop was abandoned in the reign of Cnut.

The last heard of the 'castle' was in 1209 when the sum of 40 marks (£26.80p) was paid 'towards the building work at the castle of Cadbury' to Peter de Scudamore and Godfrey de St Martin. These two were West-Country men, but whether this Cadbury is meant is not at all certain; and what they built has not been found.

Source: L. Alcock, *By South Cadbury is that Camelot*.

Access: private farmland. There is a public footpath from South Cadbury village, its start marked by an explanatory board. The path climbs towards the summit of the hill but turns to the right and passes around the base of the fortifications. Access to the summit is permitted by the landowner.

LANGPORT   Centred on ST422268

Langport was first mentioned as one of the tenth-century chain of fortresses or fortified towns created to defend Wessex against Danish invasion by Edward the Elder. By about 930 coins were being minted there, and very soon the settlement on the fortified hill spread down towards the River Parrett. Land called Beneathwall and Roughdich, mentioned in the mid fourteenth century, indicate that the town had been defended in the medieval period, and

Hanging Chapel, Langport, 1850

the medieval Hanging Chapel is the only surviving gateway.

The hilltop was fortified again during the Civil War when in June 1643 the Royalists garrisoned the town.

Source: *V. C. H. Somerset*, iii. 16, 21.

Access: the best parts of the defences are to be seen in the private grounds of the St Gildas Centre, opposite the church.

LYNG, EAST   Village centred on ST333289; fort ST342292

In 878 King Alfred built a stronghold (*geweorc*) on the western end of Athelney island. Probably before 893 another fortress was built at the end of the adjoining ridge, 'very strong' and 'of most beautiful workmanship', joined by a bridge to the first across the river which then flowed between them. The second fortress is now represented by the village of East Lyng. Traces of a defensive bank and ditch may be seen west of the village, enough to identify it with one of the *burhs* listed in the Burghal Hidage, part of the line of defences of Saxon Wessex established by Edward the Elder.

Source: *V. C. H. Somerset*, vi. 53; *Proc. Som. Arch. Soc.* cxi. 64-6.

Access: Lyng lies on the A361 Taunton-Glastonbury road; the minor road from the east end of the village to Athelney runs along the causeway which replaced the Saxon bridge between the two strongholds and skirts the south side of the island.

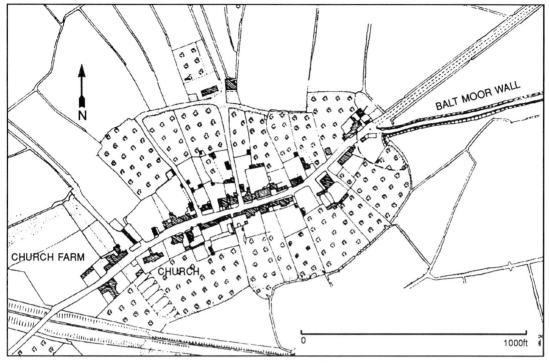

Lyng: plan of burh

WATCHET
ST061432

Excavation suggests that the original earthwork defences on the cliff top west of Watchet belong to the time of King Alfred (871-99) or of Edward the Elder (899-925). The defences were strengthened with a mortared stone wall, possibly in connection with Danish raids in the early tenth century. At the east end of the defences stood a church, probably dedicated to St Decuman, its site remembered in the name Old Minster given to one of the adjacent fields. A mint in the *burh* was producing coins from *c.* 980 but not after 1056. A tax paid in 1086 by Old Cleeve and Williton manors had perhaps begun as a charge for manning or maintaining the defences.

Coastal erosion threatened the *burh*. The town of Watchet developed at the mouth of the Washford river and the church was rebuilt on a safer site, probably in the thirteenth century. The bones of St Decuman, the church's Celtic patron, were translated to the new site on a feast still commemorated in the sixteenth century. The cliff-top site was abandoned to farming. About 1537 Thomas Dawe occupied part of the hill, then still called *le castell*.

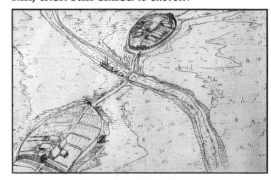

*Lyng and Athelney:
reconstruction by Mick Aston*

Source: *V. C. H. Somerset*, v. 146, 165; *Proc. Som. Arch. Soc.* cxxx. 47-60.

Access: beside road between Watchet and Carhampton.

CASTLES

BRENT MARSH

In 1189 Richard Cotele, one of Glastonbury abbey's most prominent tenants, did homage for a *castellarium* in the manor of Brent Marsh. Elias Cotele, son of Richard, granted it with his mother's consent to Robert, son of Thomas de la Pulle. From Thomas it passed to Reginald de Mere and Reginald gave it in 1270 to Abbot Robert of Petherton.

The name Brent Marsh implies a site on the low-lying land east or south of Brent Knoll; no such site has yet been found.

Source: *Liber Henrici de Soliaco Abbatis Glaston.*, ed. J.E. Jackson (Roxburgh Club 1882), 5; *Custumaria of Glastonbury Abbey*, ed. C.I. Elton (Somerset Record Soc. v), 4, 233; *Feodary of Glastonbury Abbey*, ed. F.W. Weaver (Somerset Record Soc. xxvi), 96-7.

BRIDGWATER   Centred on ST299372

William Brewer (died 1226), lord of the manor of Bridgwater, was licensed in 1200 by King John to build a castle. In the same year other charters established a weekly market and annual fair there, and declared the settlement a free borough, thus creating a new town on the west bank of the Parrett, on a small ridge which pottery found there suggests had been used a thousand

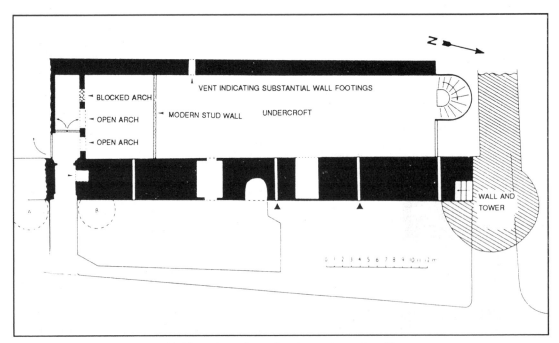

Bridgwater: plan of water gate and wall

years earlier. Brewer was also granted the right of pontage in 1200, that is the power to raise money to build and maintain the bridge which was crucial to the success of the new town.

The castle, on the highest part of the little ridge, was roughly rectangular and occupied the north-east quarter of the town. On its north side was a ditch fed with water diverted from the Durleigh Brook and filled from the river at high tide. On its east was the river, the bank later occupied by a quay. On the south and west, beyond a ditch, was the town.

Very little remains of Brewer's castle above ground – the water gate, part of a circular tower and a length of thick curtain wall, all on the river side. Between the death of Brewer's son, also William, in 1233 and 1248 when ownership passed to Maud de Braose, wife of Roger de Mortimer (died 1282), the Crown used the castle as a store and prison and in 1242 paid the constable for repairs to the mound on which the keep stood and some turrets, and in 1246 to roof the towers and renew a palisade. The Crown again occupied the castle between 1322 and 1326 lest another Roger Mortimer should escape from the Tower of London and use it as a base for operations in Wales. At this time it was again a prison and was defended by four men-at-arms and 18 cross-bow men and archers.

For some years before 1360 the Mortimers neglected the castle and it was described as a ruin, only St Mark's chapel and a barn having been repaired in the 1340s. By that time some of the moat had been filled and built over, but there was still water on the south side. It served as a useful link between the Mortimer estates in Wales and the West Country, and repairs were again put in hand to make it a place for safe storage.

Accounts for the 1380s and 1390s record repairs to towers and to the then still impressive main entrance, a great gatehouse on the town side of the moat leading from the Cornhill opening on a drawbridge, then a barbican and outer

Bridgwater: the mansion on the site of the keep, c. 1800

bailey, another bridge and the inner bailey. Within the walls (there was a stout oak palisade on the north side) stood Mortimer's Hall, the constable's lodge, the chapel, a kitchen, stable, barn, pigeon house, horse mill, cellar and dungeon. By this date the hall and dungeon were both used for farm storage. The only vaguely military connection was that the bailey was sometimes used for archery practice; in 1408 it was noted in the local court that three men had taken away two guns.

By the 1450s private houses had been built within the walls and houses on the north side of Fore Street had extended over the moat. Before 1502 there were buildings each side of the main gate and in the 1540s Leland wrote that the castle was 'all going to mere ruin'. There was still a constable and a bailiff of the ditches, and until about 1607 a castle keeper, but in 1548 what was described as 'the old frame of the castle', perhaps a timber hall, had fallen down and had been removed. Other buildings within the walls, it was suggested in 1565, might be demolished to provide a site and materials for a customs house and a new quay.

The site was thus presumably open, but some outer walls were still standing although the then owner, Henry Harvey, pulled down some in the early 1630s and the buildings seem to have been of little use during the Civil War. Still, in 1650 a nervous government thought it might have military value and insisted that the town be strongly garrisoned.

In the later seventeenth century John Harvey built a mansion on the summit of the site, its western front in the form of a twin-towered gatehouse. In 1720 eight rooms on the first floor were occupied by the estate steward and later by a schoolmistress. At the same time the land between it and the east curtain wall was developed by the duke of Chandos who began building the present Chandos and Castle streets. In 1726 the castle wall was breached to allow both streets access to the quay. Late in the eighteenth century plans were drawn up for buildings on the western part of the site which for long was pitted open ground and gardens. The mansion was subsequently demolished and King Square was laid out in the early nineteenth century.

Sources: *V. C. H. Somerset*, vi. 206-7; *Proc. Som. Arch. Soc.* cxxxv. 169.

Access: to water gate in West Quay; display in King Square.

BURY CASTLE,   SS938269
Brompton Regis

The motte-and-bailey earthwork known as Bury castle was declared by Collinson to have been built by 'the family of Besills', whom he knew to have been owners of the manor of Brompton Regis in the fourteenth century. They were not, however, owners at the time when such strongholds were being constructed.

The lord of most of the land at Domesday (1086) was the king himself, but for almost a century thereafter the ownership is unknown. In 1198 Richard I confirmed that Brompton should be part of the inheritance of Maud, one of the two daughters of William de Say the younger (died 1177). Her sister Beatrice, who had recently died, had been wife of Geoffrey FitzPeter, the powerful earl of

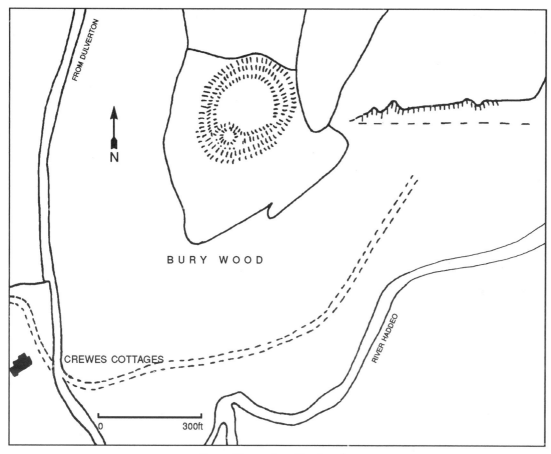

Bury, Brompton Regis: plan

Essex. Maud herself was married to William de Bochlaunde. William de Say, father of Maud and Beatrice was the elder son of another William de Say who had died in 1144. His mother was Beatrice, sister of the powerful and treacherous Geoffrey de Mandeville, earl of Essex (d. 1144), and grand-daughter of the first Geoffrey de Mandeville, builder of the great castle of Pleshey in Essex.

The builder of Bury castle is not known, but the elder William de Say, brother-in-law of one of the leading protagonists in the civil war of Stephen's reign, is a likely candidate. Since he died in 1144 the fortification may well be contemporary with Castle Cary.

The site, now covered in trees in Bury wood, is on the top of a spur above the Haddeo river. The motte is at the slightly lower southern edge of the circular bailey.

Source: *Ancient Charters* (Pipe Roll Soc. x), 108.

Access: private.

CASTLE BATCH, Worle   ST363638

Worle was the first of Walter of Douai's estates to be listed in Domesday Book.

There is some doubt about the fortification, a large mound with a hollow in it which may be the remains of a large stone tower, and a possible bailey. It stood overlooking the Levels opposite a similar site belonging to the bishop of Coutances. A little more than a century later the estate belonged to William de Courtenay. By 1303 it was held by John de Beauchamp of William de Boys.

Source: *The Archaeology of Avon*, 123.

Access: by footpath.

CASTLE CARY   ST642322

According to Domesday Book the estate called *Cari* belonged to William of Douai, lord of vast estates in the West Country. His son Robert of Bampton, whose castle at Bampton (Devon) is still to be seen, probably also built other strongholds both here at Cary and at East Harptree. Robert, according to one chronicler, was not a pleasant character: in peacetime he was said to have been 'devoted only to gluttony and drunkenness'; after the death of Henry I he assumed 'a spirit of rebellion'. As a consequence he was exiled in 1136 by Stephen and his castles passed to other hands.

In the civil war which followed, the new owners, William FitzJohn at Harptree and Ralph Lovel at Cary, both took up arms against the king and sided with Robert, earl of Gloucester. From these two strongholds they ravaged the countryside as the king laid siege to Bristol. Stephen thus abandoned the siege and 'very quickly ... with vigour and determination' attacked Cary castle with fire and showers of stones from his engines until rations ran short inside and the defenders surrendered.

Thereafter, all was apparently peaceful until 1143 when Stephen seems to have lost control of the West Country after the battle of Wilton. Four years later, after the death of Robert of Gloucester, Henry de Tracy built another stronghold in front of the older castle, thus effectively keeping the garrison inside. However, the new earl of Gloucester 'arrived suddenly with a mighty host, levelled to the ground what Henry had begun, and compelled him and his men to a shameful retreat'. Thus, it seems, ended the military history of the castle.

The Lovels eventually secured the return of the fortress and held it until the middle of the fourteenth century. During that time it was, in feudal language, the head of an 'honor', successive members of the family owing an agreed number of knights for royal service or their cash equivalent. Whether the castle continued in use is not certain. When farm buildings were altered in the 1970s a few fragments of pottery were found from the twelfth, thirteenth and fourteenth centuries. The only excavation of the site, undertaken in 1890, uncovered a large and very substantial stone keep, almost 78ft square with walls 15ft thick. Sling stones, a spear head and animal bones were found, but nothing to suggest any later history. Worked stone, either in situ or found re-used in walls and houses in the town, was quarried at Doulting and on Ham Hill, some evidence of an expensive undertaking. A very wide and deep ditch was noticed in the 1970s.

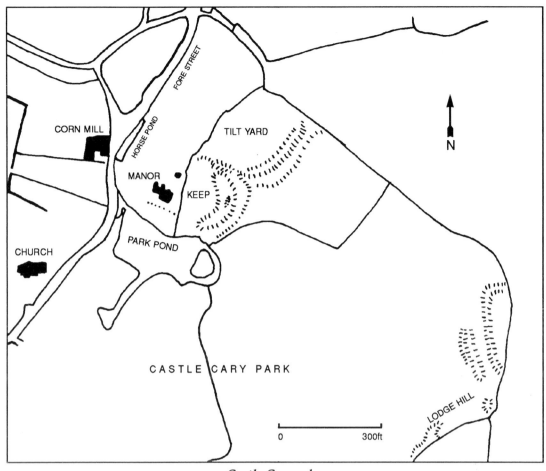

Castle Cary: plan

From the Lovel family the town and castle passed to the Seymours and later to the Zouches. The Zouches are said to have built a house within the castle precinct. John, Lord Zouche, was attainted for his support of Richard III at Bosworth and Castle Cary passed to Sir William Willoughby (died 1513) and then to his nephew Robert, Lord Willoughby de Broke (died 1521). The property came to the Seymours again in the person of Edward Seymour, duke of Somerset, and his descendants, but the house was occupied in the 1630s by Edward Kirton. It was largely demolished at the end of the eighteenth century but 'several fine old arches' then still remained.

Sources: *Gesta Stephani*, edited K.R. Potter, new introduction by R.H.C. Davis (1976); *Proc. Som. Arch. Soc.* xxxvi. 168-74.

Access: by path from main street towards private farmland.

CASTLE NEROCHE, ST271159
Staple Fitzpaine

Excavations on the site of Castle Neroche in the 1960s suggested four phases of development of a complex earthwork, three of which were after 1066. Of the three phases, the first was a small enclosure, a simple military base within earlier defences perhaps to be associated with operations during the English revolt against the Conqueror in 1067-9. The second phase was its conversion to a motte-and-bailey castle, on a large scale which must have been the work of a man of status and substance. The obvious candidates for owner and builder are Robert, Count of Mortain, half brother of the Conqueror, or his son William.

Archaeologists found traces of a stone curtain wall around the summit of the motte, surrounding a small stone 'shell'

Castle Neroche: reconstruction by Mick Aston

keep. It was thought at the time that the motte must have been built before 1088 and that the buildings on it belonged to the early twelfth century. A fourth phase of occupation was assumed to be associated with the disturbed reign of Stephen (1135-54), although no owner could be identified.

The creation or extension of Neroche Forest in the later twelfth century may have given the fortress some continued use by the administrators of the forest, who may have used it as a base for their protective operations against poachers of vert and venison or as a vantage point for those legally entitled to hunt there.

Source: *Proc. Som. Arch. Soc. cxvi. 16-58.*

Access: the earthworks lie in woodland now forming part of the modern Neroche Forest administered by the Forestry Commission. A waymarked walk passes over the castle mound and across some of the other fortifications.

CROFT CASTLE, Crewkerne ST421108

About 1150 Baldwin de Redvers, earl of Devon, gave to the bishop of Salisbury, his neighbour on the north Dorset boundary, the services of some knights who had previously been in some way attached to his castle at Crewkerne. Three of the knights were local men: from Seaborough, Chedington and Wambrook. Perhaps they or their tenants had formerly helped to build and defend it.

Baldwin had inherited the manor of Crewkerne from his father Richard, to whom Henry I had granted it before 1107. Either Richard or Baldwin is likely to have built the castle. Baldwin died in 1155 and after the deaths of his elder son and two grandsons, the manor passed in 1193 to his younger son William, earl of Devon and lord of the

Croft, Crewkerne

Isle of Wight. William died in 1217 and his estate was divided between his two daughters, Joan, wife of William Brewer (died 1233), receiving land in a place called Cruft which was also described as land 'of the castles'. In 1256 Joan gave some of her land to Christchurch priory, and the charter recording the gift was dated at her home at Craft.

By 1267 Joan had been succeeded by Isabel de Forz, countess of Devon and Aumale, and this part of her huge estate came to be called Craft Comitisse, 'Countess's Craft'. An account of the income and expenditure on the countess's manor of Craft and Cruk for the year 1267-8 survives in the Bodleian Library in Oxford. It is mostly con-cerned with rents, the sale of crops and stock and with payments of wages to servants, but it also includes evidence of preparations made for a visit the countess was to pay: two vats mended, wood collected for brewing and baking, and 39 gallons of wine bought. Where she and her retinue stayed is not exactly stated, and after they had departed her bailiff sold off a small cask and 100 gallons of ale. The dwelling, whatever it was, was obviously not in regular use and the old countess was not expected again. In the absence of any other manor house on the estate, the countess's temporary lodging must have been the family castle.

The site of the castle, in the extreme

Culverhay, Englishcombe

north-west of Crewkerne parish and overlooking Hinton St George, was known in the seventeenth century as 'the castles' and is now called Castle Hill. On its flat summit, which provides a fine view north to Ham Hill and Ilchester, worked Ham stone and twelfth-century pottery have been found.

Sources: *Proc. Som. Arch. Soc.* cxxi. 129-30; *Transactions of the Royal Historical Society* 5th series, 34, 137-8.

Access: private farmland.

CULVERHAY, Englishcombe   ST719630

A small excavation carried out on a tongue of land above the Padleigh Brook some 400 yards east of Englishcombe church revealed the base of a small circular stone keep and a larger surrounding ringwork forming a roughly oval bailey or courtyard with internal stone revetment, probably the remains of a stone curtain wall. The only finds recorded were roofing tiles; there was an ashlar-lined well. Estimates of date vary between the late eleventh and the early thirteenth century.

Nigel de Gournay was tenant there of the bishop of Coutances in 1086. Robert de Gournay was followed by his daughter Hawise and her husband Robert FitzHarding. Their daughter Eva de Gournay married Thomas of Harptree, presumably owner of Richmont castle. Until further excavation establishes a more certain date, responsibility for the foundation cannot be known.

Source: *Proc. Bath Field Club*, 1934-8,

226-30; *Archaeology of Avon*, 123-4.

Access: beside road north of Englishcombe village.

DOWNEND, Puriton   ST309414

Excavations in 1908 established that the site was occupied in the early Norman period but no castle was mentioned. A possible motte-and-bailey was later identified, linked with the earthworks of a medieval borough *de capite montis*, otherwise called *Dunevde*, mentioned in 1225. This may be the *Dunefed* where Glastonbury abbey owned four houses in the same period.

The manor was owned at Domesday by the church of St Peter in Rome and no resident tenant was named. A century later Puriton manor was owned by the Columbers family, builders of Nether Stowey and possible creators both of the borough and of the motte.

Source: *Proc. Som. Arch. Soc.* lv. 162-74; M.W. Beresford, *New Towns of the Middle Ages*, 483-4; *Custumaria of Glastonbury Abbey* (S.R.S. v), 4.

Access: the site lies beside the A38 at Dunball.

DUNSTER   SS991434

The view of Dunster castle from the distance is almost fairytale, just the purpose of Anthony Salvin's reconstruction for Mr G. F. Luttrell in the 1860s. At its core, however, it is a genuine military stronghold, built by William de Mohun before 1086 on an impregnable cliff above the valley

Dunster

where the River Avill flowed into the sea. It was a classic motte-and-bailey formed out of the natural shape of the hill, both motte and bailey so steep that it was never carried in an assault. It was defended by the second William de Mohun against King Stephen, when it was described as washed by the tide on one side and fortified by towers and walls, a rampart (*vallo*) and earthworks on the other. The towers and walls were probably on the summit of the tor which gave the castle its name in Domesday Book. The rampart and earthworks may have been a lower ward.

Reynold Mohun (died 1258) built the lower ward in stone. Soon after Reynold's death a survey of the castle listed a hall, buttery, pantry, kitchen, bakehouse, chapel, knights' hall, three towers and a prison in the upper ward, and three towers including the Fleming tower (named after Reynold's first wife) and a granary in the lower ward. One of the towers was evidently a gateway. Some of the buildings were covered in lead by the end of the thirteenth century, others were roofed with wooden shingles.

Sir Hugh Luttrell, a distinguished military figure in the French wars under Henry V, carried out considerable repairs, may have rebuilt the great hall, and certainly built the great gatehouse and barbican between 1419 and 1424. There was perhaps some neglect after 1460 when the Luttrells lost possession to the Herberts: Leland recorded that only the chapel was 'in good case' in the upper ward but that Sir Andrew Luttrell (died 1538) had built a wall on the east side.

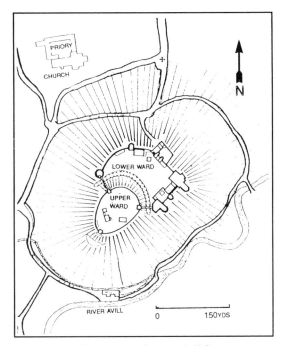

Dunster: plan, c. 1430

eventual heir, actually let part of the castle; and his son George transformed it from castle to country house. Part of the work was perhaps finished in the late 1580s; the rest was carried out to the designs of William Arnold over a period of years ending in the 1620s.

Thomas Luttrell (1584-1644) was still able to defend his home. He garrisoned it for Parliament in 1642 but yielded it in June 1643 to the Royalist Sir Francis Wyndham. Wyndham held it until April 1646, ignoring mining which destroyed part of the wall. Until 1650 it was garrisoned for Parliament and then 200 men spent twelve days demolishing walls and buildings in the upper ward and defacing the gatehouse. Only the mansion house was saved; the rest was 'so farre slighted as that it may not be made suddainely teneable by an enemy'.

Source: Maxwell-Lyte, *A History of Dunster; Proc. Som. Arch. Soc.* cxxv. 1-15.

Access: owned by National Trust.

Sir Andrew was buried not at Dunster like his predecessors but at East Quantoxhead, where both he and his father had preferred to live in a more comfortable and modest house. In 1556 Thomas Luttrell, Sir Andrew's son and

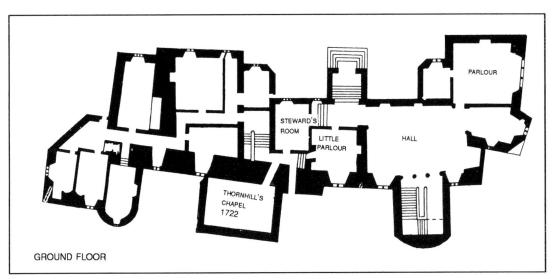

Dunster: George Luttrell's house

EDITHMEAD, Burnham   ST328493

If the earthwork is a denuded motte-and-bailey rather than a moated site, then it may perhaps have been the work of Walter of Douai or his son Robert of Bampton. Walter was lord of Burnham in 1086 and Robert remained in possession from his father's death about 1107 until his own rebellion in 1136 when he was succeeded by his daughter Juliana. It may be of interest that the owners from the late twelfth century were the descendants of Harold son of Ralph who in the time of William Rufus had owned the great castle of Ewyas Harold in Herefordshire.

Source: Sanders, *English Baronies*, 5, 43; *Historical Manuscripts Commission, Wells Cathedral MSS*, i, 47, 229, 454.

Access: in Edithmead hamlet.

LOCKING HEAD, Locking   ST364609

Locking is not mentioned in Domesday Book. Some scholars have suggested it was part of Woodspring (Kewstoke) manor and thus belonged to William of Falaise. Others believe it to have formed part of Hutton, where one manor was held directly of the king by the bishop of Coutances and the other by the bishop as subtenant of Glastonbury abbey. The two manors were evidently united, reverted to the Crown and were given by Henry I to Geoffrey de Dun. In 1214 Locking was given by Geoffrey Gibwyne, who held it of the Courtenay family, to the canons of Woodspring priory.

The site, on a low hill commanding, with Castle Batch in Worle, a possible entrance to the Levels, is a small motte-and-bailey built against an earlier deep hollow way. All military significance would have disappeared after acquisition by the canons.

Source: *Archaeology of Avon*, 123-4.

Access: visible from footpath between Drove and Locking Head farms.

MONTACUTE   ST494170

According to Domesday Book, Robert, count of Mortain and half-brother of William the Conqueror, held an estate called 'Biscopeston', to which was attached a castle called 'Montagud'. The site had been chosen deliberately: the monks of Athelney had been the owners before the Conquest, and before them the monks of Glastonbury, one of whose abbots, Tunbeorht, became bishop of Winchester – hence the name Biscopeston. The original village street still bears the name Bishopston. An even earlier name was Logworesbeorh, mentioned in a Glastonbury charter of the seventh century.

So the place had strong Saxon traditions, and the arrival of a Norman conqueror, making his presence felt by the construction of a castle on a natural hill overlooking the village, posed a challenge which even after the defeat at Hastings was not to be borne. It was not simply a castle in their midst, but a castle built on a hill where only recently a fragment of the True Cross had miraculously been found. The relic,

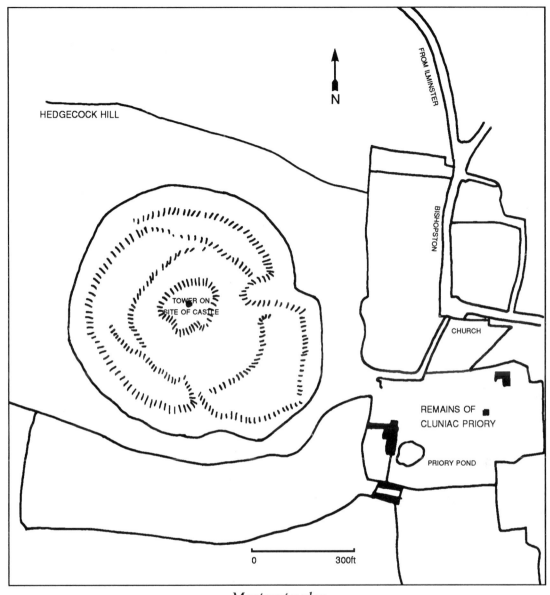

Montacute: plan

taken to Waltham in Essex and venerated as the English battle-cry at Hastings, had lost none of its appeal to the defeated. So, in 1068 the new castle was under siege by English rebels until the arrival of superior forces under Bishop Geoffrey of Coutances.

The castle was created from a conical hill scarped to form an oval motte with an upper bailey to the south-east and a lower bailey on a plateau encircling the hill. William, count of Mortain, the builder's son, was forced to surrender his lands about 1100 and soon afterwards gave it to the newly-founded Cluniac priory he had built below the castle near the village church. At the time the castle included a chapel

41

Montacute

dedicated to St Michael, reached by a flight of stone steps. The chapel continued to be used until the beginning of the fourteenth century or later, but presumably the monks had little use for a castle. Yet although it was certainly used as a convenient source for cut stone – two loads were sold to the churchwardens of Tintinhull in 1518-19 – it was still described in the 1630s as 'a fine piece of work built with arched work, and an embowned roof, overlaid all of stone, very artificially'.

In the eighteenth century the castle mound provided a fashionable prospect from Montacute House. A tower was built on the summit in 1760 which affords a wonderful view. Trees were first planted later in the century.

Source: *V.C.H. Somerset*, iii. 215.

Access: by footpath.

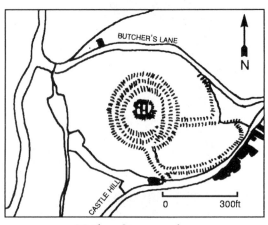

Nether Stowey: plan

42

NETHER STOWEY   ST186387

In 1166 Philip de Columbers owned an estate called the 'honor' of Nether Stowey, to which ten knights owed service. Among them were the owners of manors at Spaxton, Goathurst, Otterhampton, Plainsfield, Woolmersdon in North Petherton, and Stockland Lovel. Philip's wife Maud was the daughter of Walter de Chandos, himself grandson of Alfred d'Epaignes, owner of Stowey in 1086. Probably Walter (died by 1156) or his father Robert (died 1120) had abandoned their castle at Over Stowey (*below*) in favour of a new site west of Nether Stowey village, from which there was a better view of the coast. The Columbers family continued until 1342 when ownership of Nether Stowey passed to the Audleys. Long before that time the

Nether and Over Stowey

Over Stowey

castle had lost any military significance. In 1485 the site was being used for grazing cattle.

The castle comprised a steep-sided motte and two baileys. A small stone keep stood on the motte, and the outline of its foundations can still be seen. The baileys, surrounded by ditches, have both been quarried for stone.

Source: *V.C.H. Somerset*, v. 194-5.

Access: by footpath.

OVER STOWEY   ST187396

In 1086 Alfred d'Epaignes, sometimes called Alfred of Spain, held several estates on the Quantocks including one called Stowey of which Harold, earl of Wessex, had once been owner. The description of the estate included the usual arable, meadow and pasture and, of course, several villagers; but there is no mention of a castle.

In the mid twelfth century Hugh de Bonville, who had succeeded his father Hamon and his grandfather Ralph in this part of Alfred's estate, gave to the church of Over Stowey a piece of land. Part of the boundary of that land followed a road, already ancient, called the Stowey Harepath, which in Stowey ran by the 'old castle'. A field between the harepath and the church was still called Castle Close in the nineteenth century.

A large, flat mound is still to be seen in this field, providing a good view towards the mouth of the River Parrett. Alfred d'Epaignes's daughter Isabel, wife of Robert de Chandos, succeeded her father and Robert (died 1120) or his son Walter (died by 1156) evidently decided that a better site was to be had further north at Nether Stowey (*above*). Over Stowey was abandoned.

Incidentally, Over Stowey was fortified again in 1645 when the royalist rector, John Selleck, may have strengthened the church tower as well as the rectory house in the king's cause.

Source: *V.C.H. Somerset*, vi. 160.

Access: private farmland; site visible from road.

RICHMONT, East Harptree   ST561558

East Harptree like Cary belonged in 1086 to the great landowner Walter of Douai, and it seems likely that its castle was built by his son Robert of Bampton. It may have been involved in Robert's rebellion against Stephen in 1136, but two years later it was under the control of William FitzJohn, a loyal supporter of Robert, earl of Gloucester. William, like Ralph Lovel at Cary, was a threat to King Stephen, then attempting to besiege Robert in Bristol, and after successful action against Ralph, Stephen turned to deal with Harptree. His first plan was to build a siege work against it, but in the event decided to control it with troops based at Bath.

John Leland, writing in the early sixteenth century, believed that someone he described simply as 'Gurney', founder of the priory of nuns at Barrow Gurney who was buried at Stoke, had built the castle. He must have been thinking of Sir Matthew Gournay, a famous soldier who fought at Crecy and Poitiers and who took a prominent part in military and diplomatic affairs at the end of the fourteenth century. He could claim to be founder of the nunnery at Barrow since he was a direct descendant of an unknown Gurney, probably in the late twelfth century. Sir Matthew was certainly buried in the chapel of his fortified manor house at Stoke sub Hamdon (*see below*) in 1406.

A map of the later sixteenth century depicts a fanciful Gothic building which at least may have reminded people of the home Sir Matthew often stayed at. After Gournay's death without children the estate passed to the Newtons. In the 1540s what Leland called the 'dungeon', presumably the keep, was still standing but Sir John Newton had already decided to build a new house at Eastwood and had dug up the foundations of some of the already ruined castle. Stone walling could still be seen in the seventeenth century on the spur overlooking a deep and narrow valley, but the site has evidently been disturbed by lead mining. It is now covered with trees but open to visitors.

Sources: Leland, *Itinerary*, v. 85, 104-5; *Gesta Stephani*, ed. K. R. Potter.

Access: by footpath through woodland.

STOGURSEY   ST203426

Stogursey castle stands a little distance south of the centre of Stogursey village and is now owned by the Landmark Trust which has restored the building and leases the tiny house to holiday makers. The castle at its greatest extent comprised a mound on which the surviving buildings stand, now surrounded by a moat. Further protection was given by two baileys, one on the south and east, the other, slightly higher, further east. Both are marked out by banks and watercourses. There is another enclosure surrounded by a bank to the north and east.

During its restoration in the 1980s the site was partially excavated and Richard McDonnell, in charge of the work,

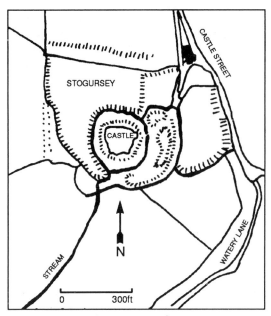

Stogursey: plan

found evidence beneath the castle mound which suggested an earlier dwelling, perhaps the house William de Falaise referred to in his charter to the abbey of Lonlay near his home in Normandy soon after the year 1100.

William's daughter Emma married the first William de Curci and their grandson, also William de Curci, in 1166 was described as holding the barony of Stogursey. It seems very likely that there was a castle here by 1166.

The curtain wall contains work of the twelfth century, but there is no reference to a building until 1204. (The claims that a castle was there in 1090 is a mistake for the castle at Curci-sur-Dives in Calvados.)

Owners of the castle after the Curcis were not always loyal to the Crown. In 1216 when Warin FitzGerold was out of favour, orders were given to destroy the building. The next owner, Fawkes de Breaute, also rebelled and the castle was besieged and in 1224 given up to the king. Fawkes's successor, on the king's side, was ordered in 1233 to fortify it, and the present towers are probably the result, the gatehouse built in place of a single tower. Seventy years later, when the castle was again in the control of the king, the constable was ordered to repair the bridges over the moat.

In 1308 the castle came into the hands of Robert FitzPayn of Poorstock, Dorset, and was held by his descendants, from 1394 the lords Poynings, from 1484 earls of Northumberland. For long it had ceased to have any military significance

Stogursey, 1733

(statements about a siege and destruction in 1457 by Lord Bonville are quite without foundation) but in the 1490s, when it was owned by Henry Algernon Percy, earl of Northumberland, a new tower was built and others were repaired so that the castle could be used by John Parker, the constable, who administered the estates of the earl at Stogursey and Cannington. One of the new rooms fitted out was an audit room complete with a 'chequerboard', another was a wardrobe for storage, and a third was a prison. There was also new living accommodation for the steward, including a nursery.

Repairs were occasionally made between that date and 1519, and a man was paid as constable until 1530-1, but no estate official seems to have lived there after Parker. The building was said in 1538 to be in decay, and later in the sixteenth century rabbits were bred within the walls. The present house was made out of the gatehouse before 1614 and was rebuilt in 1878.

Source: *V.C.H. Somerset*, vi. 136-7.

Access: by footpath; regularly let to tenants by Landmark Trust.

Stogursey: the gatehouse

TAUNTON   ST226246

According to the Anglo-Saxon Chronicle under the year 722 'Queen Aethelburh demolished Taunton, which Ine had built'. Scholars consider that some sort of stronghold rather than a complete settlement is here referred to, a stronghold presumably raised by the advancing Saxons under Ine himself after the defeat of the British king Geraint in 710. No trace of the fortress has yet been found. It had been thought to mark the beginning of the medieval castle at Taunton; it could as well be, for instance, on the high ground above the River Tone at Bishops Hull.

The present castle site was of ecclesiastical and not military significance, for there stood a minster church and its dependent buildings, perhaps founded in the eighth century. The first direct and contemporary reference to the castle is in the Annals of Winchester for the year 1138, where it occurs among the list of buildings of Henry of Blois, bishop of Winchester (1129-71), a key figure in Stephen's reign. An alternative theory suggests it was the work of Henry's predecessor as bishop, William

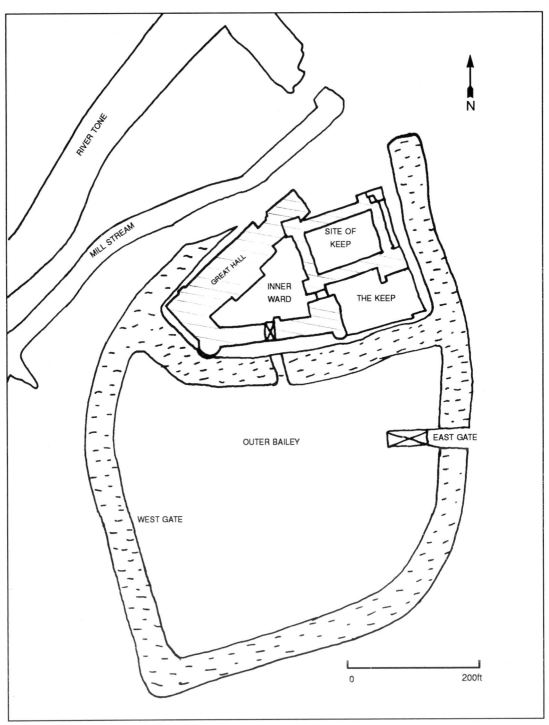

Taunton: plan

Giffard, who had control of the estates of the see from 1100.

By the later twelfth century the castle comprised a substantial rectangular

Taunton: the keep under excavation, c. 1926

keep measuring about 65 feet by 98 feet, a first-floor great hall over a stone vaulted undercroft and, at right angles to it, a chamber block. Early in the thirteenth century, at a time of potential civil war and possible French invasion, Bishop Peter des Roches, King John's Justiciar, had both castle and town surrounded with ditches. The cost of the ditching was nearly £67, and of other work by carpenters and masons over £57. Visitors in Bishop Peter's time (1206-38) included King John, Queen Isabella and the young Henry III. Thirty years later Bishop William Raleigh (1240-50) made considerable alterations, creating a ground-floor hall in Ham stone, strengthening the chamber block, and building a new kitchen and chapel.

The castle was prepared for trouble during the Barons' War of the 1260s (680 crossbow bolts cost 5s 8d) and was used as a prison for the safe keeping of Simon de Montfort's son until 1282. Disaster struck from natural causes in 1326 when the whole site was flooded, and newly-dug ditches and sluice gates provided later in the century suggests a continuing problem. In 1451 the defences were at last tested when the earl of Devon besieged Lord Bonville.

By this date the castle was arranged around two baileys. The inner comprised the keep or great tower with its hall and quarters for soldiers, topped by five turrets, one of which served as a prison. Between the keep and the great hall once stood the kitchen with a tower above it, facing the river. This kitchen was replaced by a new one and other domestic quarters such as a bakehouse, buttery and pantry in Bishop Raleigh's time, but the tower remained, together with a bridge leading to a garden behind the keep. Adjoining the hall was the range which included the bishop's chamber on the first floor above a vaulted undercroft, a round tower with latrines, and then the chapel, also on the first floor. Next was the inner gate, with the exchequer above, refitted by Bishop Thomas Langton in 1496.

The outer bailey was larger in area and was dominated by the east gate, where the constable or his deputy lived, with rooms for guards and possibly for estate officials. Opposite was the west gate. Within the bailey were two barns, a cowshed, stables, a granary, a dairy, a dovecote and stores, together with the chapel of St Peter. The last building to be erected within the surrounding walls was a schoolhouse, paid for by Bishop Richard Fox in 1521-3.

For most of its history until the sixteenth century the castle had served as the centre for the administration of the vast local estates of the bishops of Winchester. Thereafter it was maintained for a variety of public uses and was effectively under the control of successive bailiffs or keepers. In 1635 it was described as 'much ruinated' but some money was spent there at the outbreak of the Civil War in 1642 and both castle and town were garrisoned by Parliament in 1643. Lost and recaptured again it suffered damage when Robert Blake defended it, and parts were later sold off, while orders were given that the keep should be demolished.

The great hall, regularly used for assizes and other courts from the sixteenth century, was the scene of one of the sessions of the Bloody Assize in 1685 when 144 followers of the duke of Monmouth were sentenced to be hanged and 284 to be transported. The hall was divided into two court rooms and other offices in the 1780s and then and about 1816 it was largely rebuilt. Assizes continued to be held there until 1857. During the same period the remaining buildings were in use as private dwellings and a school and surviving walls were incorporated in what became the Castle Hotel and the Winchester Arms inn. After 1857 the hall was used for public entertainments and political meetings.

The Somerset Archaeological Society bought the castle in 1874 and installed their museum in the hall. The castle today still belongs to the Society, but much of it is now occupied by the Somerset County Museum, whose displays are to be found in the former great hall and the bishop's chamber range as well as in galleries added during the present century. The site of the keep is let to the Castle Hotel as a garden. The former chapel and its undercroft, the exchequer and the round tower adjoining the chamber range are occupied by the Archaeological Society.

Taunton: the east gate

Source: *The Archaeology of Taunton*, ed. P. Leach, 11-58.

Access: to the Somerset County Museum (admission charge); to the rooms of the Archaeological Society either through membership of the Society or by arrangement with the Secretary.

WINCANTON ST746323

In Cockroad wood, now in Charlton Musgrove but in the ancient parish of Wincanton. The motte, with a rectangular bailey to the south and a possibly earlier triangular ringwork to the north-west, stands on a strongly defensive site on the west side of the Selwood ridge.

Walter of Douai was the Domesday lord of Wincanton; the tenancy of Renewer was probably short-lived after 1086. Walter died about 1107 and was probably succeeded by Ralph Lovel (flourished 1121), Baldwin Lovel (dead by 1138) and another Ralph (died about 1161). Walter of Douai is the most likely builder.

Source: *V.C.H.* draft history of Wincanton.

Access: private.

Wincanton: motte-and-bailey in Cockroad wood

SOME FORTIFIED HOUSES AND MOATED SITES

BLACKFORD, Wedmore   ST410478

The bishops of Bath and Wells had an estate at Blackford by the thirteenth century and in the early fourteenth the manor house there was often used by Bishop John Droxford. The buildings were said to have been 'on a sumptuous scale' and costly to repair, and Bishop John Harewell (1369-86) demolished them. Materials still remained on the site in 1391.

Excavations in 1955-7 confirmed use of the site between the twelfth and fourteenth centuries. A moat surrounded an area about 300ft across. Only the east and west sides survive in an orchard locally known as 'The Bishop's Palace'. Judging by the character of the remaining artefacts the buildings may have been half-timbered and were roofed with brown and green glazed tiles.

Source: *Historical MSS Commission, Wells Cathedral MSS.*, i. 147, 167-8, 180, 204-6, 303; *Proc. Som. Arch. Soc.* cvii. 72-8.

Access: private.

CLEVEDON COURT,   ST423716
Clevedon

About 1320 Sir John de Clevedon transformed his home from what seems to have been something like a castle to a more domestic dwelling. Possibly some of the older building had to be demolished; what survives in the north-east corner of the present house is a rectangular, four-storeyed tower of the mid thirteenth century and a large, rectangular building at an angle to the south-west corner of the tower, added about 1300.

The new house was not entirely domestic in character: there are grooves for portcullises in both entrance porches, but they are likely to have been more symbolic than serious. Part of the garden wall aligned with the west wall of the tower may be part of the earliest, military building.

Source: *Clevedon Court* (National Trust Guide, 1969).

Access: National Trust, open.

COMBE FLOREY, Manor House
ST152312

The great, red stone gatehouse was originally four-storeyed. It contains fine plasterwork in the Great Chamber including an overmantel with the impressive achievement of arms of John Frauncis and the date 1593. The work was probably done by Robert Eaton of Stogursey. Nothing remains of the house to which the gatehouse gave such impressive access. It evidently stood between the gatehouse and the church, whose north aisle belonged to the lords of the manor.

Source: J. and J. Penoyre, *Decorative Plasterwork in Somerset* (1994), 72.

Access: private dwelling.

Clevedon Court

Combe Florey: gatehouse, 1835

Cothay Manor

COTHAY MANOR, Kittisford   ST085213

The Bluet family owned the estate from about 1330 and the house is usually ascribed either to Sir Walter Bluet (died 1481) or to his son Richard (died 1524). The latter is more likely in view of the survival of the arms of Richard and his wife Agnes Verney. The gatehouse to the south is buttressed and embattled with a higher stair turret; it was restored in 1926-7. In front of it flows a stream which, while not in any formal sense a moat, still gives the buildings a 'castle-like' character.

Source: *Proc. Som. Arch. Soc.* lviii. 65-6; *Country Life*, 22, 29 October, 1927.

Access: private dwelling.

COURT HOUSE, East Quantoxhead   ST136437

The south-eastern corner of Court House, built very close to the north side of the parish church, is an embattled four-storeyed tower which may be contemporary with the adjoining south wall and the short west range of the present house. The tower may relate to the gatehouse referred to in 1273. The position of the house is far more obviously defensive than domestic, for it stands on a ridge overlooking the Bristol Channel.

Source: *V.C.H. Somerset*, v. 123.

Access: private dwelling.

CUDWORTH   ST371111

Joan, widow of Matthew Esse, was licensed in 1333 to have a private chapel in her house at Cudworth. She was the daughter and heiress of Alan Furneaux and her family had held the manor since the late twelfth century. The site of her house is likely to be within the moat south of the church, with a ditch now 6 ft deep. To the west are what appear to be two fishponds whose water had been penned back on the north side by a substantial earth bank.

Source: *V.C.H. Somerset*, iv. 142-3.

Access: private farmland.

FAIRFIELD, Stogursey   ST187429

William Verney is said to have received licence about 1473 to encircle his house with a wall and seven round towers. Three of the towers survived into the eighteenth century on the boundary of a walled court east of the present house. The south-west wing of the present house includes two first-floor rooms of Verney's house with richly-decorated beams, and there is a contemporary blocked arch between the screens passage and the dining room.

Source: *V.C.H. Somerset*, vi. 140.

Access: private dwelling.

Court House, East Quantoxhead, 1845

Cudworth: moated site

FARLEIGH CASTLE, Farleigh Hungerford

ST801578

The Montfort family, owners of Farleigh from the time of William Rufus, chose for the site of their manor house what Leland called 'a rokky hill' overlooking the river Frome, which there forms the boundary between Somerset and Wiltshire, and a stream called Danes Dyke. House and estate passed from the last Montfort to the Burghersh family and in 1369-70 were bought for the sum of 1,000 marks (£733.33p) by Thomas Hungerford, a rising politician from Heytesbury in Wiltshire.

Within the next fourteen years or so Hungerford converted the house into a castle, for at the end of 1383 he received a royal pardon for surrounding it with a wall with towers and a parapet, and strengthened on the south and west by a ditch. By this time Hungerford was a man of importance: between 1357 and 1393 he was 16 times an MP, was knighted, and in 1377 had been elected Speaker of the House of Commons. The castle was a proper home for a man with such political influence.

The new stronghold was roughly square, with circular towers at each corner, a strong gateway in the middle of the south wall and a range of buildings including a first-floor hall and solar. The new castle, much larger than the old manor house, encroached on at least one nearby building, the village church. It was presumably Sir Thomas who rebuilt it slightly further away and he was buried in it after his death in 1397.

Sir Walter Hungerford, son and successor of Sir Thomas, was also chosen as Speaker of the House of Commons, fought at Agincourt, and was a loyal servant to both Henry V and Henry VI. In 1426 he became Baron Hungerford. About 1425, possibly out of the ransom he received from the duke of Orleans, he almost doubled the size of the castle by creating a polygonal outer court with two gatehouses and a large tower, all encircled with a dry ditch. The parish church was now within the castle and became immediately the castle chapel.

Leland described the towers of the outer court as 'praty', the gatehouse of the inner court as 'fair' and the hall and three chambers there as 'stately'. At about the time of his visit the castle was forfeit to the Crown because of the attainder and execution of Walter, Lord Hungerford, in 1540. A contemporary

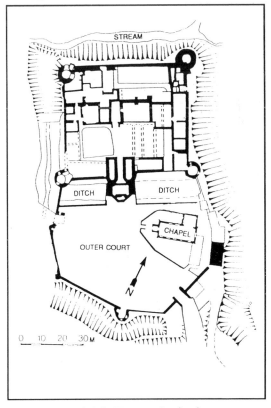

Farleigh Hungerford: plan

57

Farleigh Hungerford

survey mentioned 'fair' chambers and lodgings, and described the whole as 'portly and very strongly buylded'.

The castle was garrisoned for the king for a short time during the Civil War, and in 1644 was used for storing uniforms. A year later it surrendered without a fight; it could hardly have been held against cannon placed overlooking it. It stayed occupied until the early years of the eighteenth century.

Source: J. E. Jackson, *A Guide to Farleigh Hungerford* (1879).

Access: English Heritage; open to public.

FENNY CASTLE, Wells   ST508436

Originally in Wookey parish, the natural mound rises just over 60 feet above the level of the surrounding North Moor. Tenants of the manor court in the earlier fourteenth century bore the names atte Castell or Castel and William Worcestre in 1480 saw the plan of 'all the houses and offices there'. The ruins still survived in Leland's time, and the common name then was Fenne-Castell. John Skinner, writing in 1825, reported that a local farmer had found more than 20 human skeletons.

Source: William Worcestre, *Itinerary*, ed. J. Harvey, 293; *40th Annual Report, Wells Natural History and Archaeological Soc.* (1928), 41-4.

Access: private farmland, visible from road.

Fenny Castle, Wells

GLASTONBURY

Henry of Blois, abbot of Glastonbury (1126-71) and bishop of Winchester, left a formidable series of buildings, among them, according to the chronicler Adam of Domerham, 'a certain regal palace, which is called a castle (*castellum*)'. John of Glastonbury, writing a little later, described it simply as 'a beautiful and spacious palace (*palacium*)'. It is quite clear from the context of both writers that the building was within the monastic precinct, but the use of the word *castellum* has led some to believe that there was a free-standing 'castle' elsewhere in Glastonbury. It was subsequently identified as the Mound or Mount on the south-western edge of the town towards Beckery, which was for a time suggested as a motte-and-bailey or ringwork castle.

This mound was excavated in advance of its removal for industrial development and proved to be a site for early medieval iron smelting and not a castle. Abbot Henry's palace was recognised within the abbey grounds in 1978-9 where its massive wall foundations were exposed by W. J. Wedlake during his excavations of the Abbot's Hall. The surviving footings, incidentally, were covered with a layer of ash, clear trace of the fire which in 1184 destroyed the palace and most of the other standing buildings of the abbey.

Source: *Adami de Domerham Historia de Rebus gestis Glastoniensibus*, ed. T. Hearne, ii. 316; *The Chronicle of Glastonbury Abbey*, ed. J. Carley, 166; *Proc. Som. Arch. Soc.* cxxix. 37, 39.

Access: Glastonbury abbey is open to the public daily except Christmas Day.

HATCH BEAUCHAMP
possibly about ST307214

John de Beauchamp had licence from the Crown to fortify his manor house at Hatch in 1333. He died two years later, perhaps without having finished the work, and on the death of his son in 1343 the value of the building was put at nothing. A visitor in 1633 found it so ruinous that were it not then called Hatch Court it would not have been recognised as a house of importance. But the hall of the house displayed the arms of the Beauchamp family and a chapel 'on the top of the house' included the arms of their successors, the Seymours, indicating a date in the later fifteenth century. The house seems to have stood north of the church.

Source: T. Gerard, *Particular Description of Somerset* (Somerset Record Soc. xv), 14.

MARSH COURT, Wincanton ST741256

In 1280 it was agreed that the chapel of St Andrew at Marsh had been built by Richard Lovel, but whether the Richard who died in 1255 or the one who died in 1264 was not stated. The chapel implies the existence of a substantial house. Another Richard Lovel gave a feast at his house at Marsh in 1344 and a garden and dovecot mentioned there in 1351 suggest that the building complex was well established. It was said to be in ruins in the early 1540s. By that time ownership had passed from the Lovels to the Seymours and from them through Alice Seymour to the Zouches. John, Baron Zouche, was attainted after the battle of Bosworth in 1485 and the family lost possession for about sixty years. The house may well have been abandoned during that period.

The present site seems to include a double moat, probably the result of the division of the estate in the seventeenth century when houses may have been built in each half; only one house remains. Much of the site is covered by farm buildings.

Source: *Somersetshire Pleas* (Somerset Record Society xliv), 194-5; *Calendar of Inquisitions post mortem* xii, 70-1; P.R.O., C 135/113, no. 12; Leland, *Itinerary*, v. 219.

Access: private farmyard.

MARSTON MOAT,   ST767438
Marston Bigot

The site, overgrown by trees, measures 120 ft by 108 ft and is surrounded by a moat 20 ft wide. It seems to have been the dwelling of the Bigot family from before 1195 and in the reign of Edward II it was for a time forfeited when Richard Bigot fortified his house without licence and later insulted the king's messenger.

Source: J. Collinson, *History of Somerset*, ii. 213-4; *Proc. Som. Arch. Soc.* cxviii. 15.

Access: private farmland.

MERRYFIELD, Ilton ST340177

John Beauchamp of Hatch, who died in 1283, owned the capital messuage at Merryfield with a garden and dovecot. His great-granddaughter Cecily Turberville died there in 1394 and thereafter it passed to Sir John Wadham. The last Wadhams to live there were Nicholas (died 1609) and his wife Dorothy (died 1618), founders of Wadham College, Oxford. Nicholas's sister Florence married John Wyndham and her son John, who lived at Orchard Wyndham, demolished the house before his death in 1645. Some of the materials are said to have been used to build two farmhouses and an almshouse on the estate. Panelling from one of the farmhouses and two heraldic achievements carved in stone from the manor house itself were given to Wadham College by William Wyndham (died 1950).

One of the coats of arms records the marriage of Nicholas Wadham who died in 1541 and perhaps marks the last phase of building. Only a barn and the base of a tower including a loophole seems to have survived to the mid eighteenth century. The surrounding moat remains, its inner wall of mortared lias; some walling of the outer wall also remains, particularly opposite the fishpond.

Source: *Proc. Som. Arch. Soc.* lxxx. 1-10.

Access: footpath passes moat near course of disused railway.

NASH PRIORY, East Coker ST538138

This is no priory but probably two parts of a high-quality house whose hall and other domestic buildings have disappeared leaving a small gatehouse with chapel above and, to the west, a second building, possibly a guesthouse. The two surviving buildings were joined together in the nineteenth century to make a single range, and much of the architectural detail may have been recovered from the demolished hall range. Such details suggest an origin in the early years of the fifteenth century.

Thomas Gerard in the seventeenth century described it as 'an ancient gentleman's house owned by the Gaunts'; John Batten attributed it to a younger son of Sir William Courtenay, but he would have come too late to have built it.

Source: Notes (1979) by R. G. Gilson, deposited in Somerset Record Office. Batten, *Hist. Notes on S. Som.* 175, 181.

Access: private house.

NEWTON CASTLE, ST693639
Newton St Loe

A 'fair manor place like a castle' wrote Leland in 1540 of the house which had once been the chief home of the lords St Loe. C. J. Arnold excavated there between 1975 and 1979 and discovered that the site had been occupied since the twelfth century and that a substantial house had been begun in the late thirteenth or early fourteenth century.

That house, although excavations were not able to disclose the whole site, was probably arranged around a rectangular courtyard in two-storeyed ranges. Independent four-storeyed towers stood at each end of the long west range. Only one of these towers still survives, and also the impressive two-storeyed gatehouse which defended the house with portcullis and gunloop and gave access to the courtyard through a vaulted tunnel. The vault has intersecting ribs with finely-carved bosses. Worn coats of arms on the parapet of the remaining tower bear the arms of St Loe and Botreaux, successive builders and owners.

The date of the remaining tower is of the early fourteenth century, probably the work of Sir John St Loe, sheriff or deputy sheriff of Somerset and Dorset 1283-9, and MP for Somerset in 1297, who two years later served with Edward I in Scotland and who died in 1314. Another Sir John, his son or grandson, served four times in Parliament and died in 1375, leaving as sole heir a daughter Elizabeth, wife of William, Baron Botreaux.

Botreaux died in 1395 and his namesake and successor in 1462. Probably the gatehouse was built during his ownership. His heir was his daughter Margaret, widow of Robert, Lord Hungerford, whose own heir, also Robert, Lord Hungerford and Moleyns, was attainted and executed in 1463 and whose son Thomas suffered the same fate in 1468. Thus, on the death of Margaret in 1478 the owner of Newton castle was Mary, her great-grandchild, aged about ten and married to Edward Hastings, later Lord Hastings of Hungerford. Their son George succeeded to his mother's titles and to ownership of Newton on her death before 1532. He, created earl of Huntingdon in 1529, was the owner when Leland visited the castle in the

1540s. Perhaps the domestic windows in the surviving tower were inserted in place of the original narrow slit windows.

By that time the castle had long since ceased to be a principal residence of its owners. Edward Neville, later Lord Abergavenny, bought the house from the then earl of Huntingdon in 1565 and a descendant, George Neville, evidently sold it to Joseph Langton, a Bristol merchant, in 1666. A hundred years later a new house was built in another part of the estate and the old one was largely destroyed to make way for a carriage drive. But what survived became a suitable antique ruin for guests taking the air in the park, and turrets and crenellations were added to give an interesting effect.

Source: Leland, *Itinerary*, v.103; *Proc. Som. Arch. Soc.* cxxiv. 77-86.

Access: the ruins form part of the campus of the Bath College of Higher Education.

NORTON SUB HAMDON ST471159

In 1421 the king's escheator for Somerset assigned to Anne, the widow of Sir Thomas de la Pole, formerly lord of the manor of Norton sub Hamdon, her proper share in the manor house. This comprised a ground-floor room on the south of the farmyard, a first-floor room above the stable called 'le hayhous', the third part of the great garden. And that part of the garden was defined as 'that part of the garden which is on the east part of the same beginning from a certain ash tree growing in the great ditch by the entrance of the same garden, and thence stretching through the garden by a certain apple tree leaning over the ditch on the north of the same garden'. Lady Anne also received the rents of several tenants, a water mill and a third of the profits from the stone quarries.

In 1555 a survey of the manor included the 'capital messuage', that is the manor house and its site, 'situate and built by the parish church there', a field called Court Close and a dovecote. The dovecote still stands by the parish church. The moat may now be under the buildings of Court Farm.

Sources: P.R.O., C 138/54, no. 125; C. Trask, *Norton-sub-Hamdon* (1898), 57-8.

Access: private.

Sir John de la Mare, whose family had held land in Wiltshire and Somerset since the late twelfth century, was licensed in November 1373 to crenellate his dwelling house at Nunney. Sir John had spent some time abroad, pre- sumably in France fighting, and it is thought that the castle was paid for from the profits of war and was inspired by the Bastille in Paris. S. E. Rigold described the design as 'in many aspects' unique, with no exact parallels in England.

John Leland described it as a 'praty' building 'havynge at eche end by northe and southe 2. praty rownd towres gatheryd by compace to joyne in to one': in other words, a rectangular structure with round towers at each corner. A moat around the building was fed from

Newton Park: the castle gatehouse

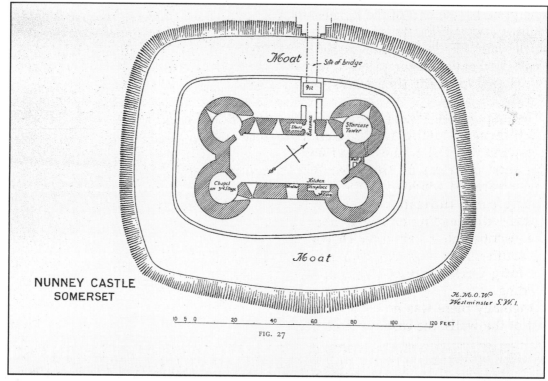

the Nunney Brook which divided the castle from the parish church yard; and beyond the moat on three sides was a 'stronge waulle' except on the church side. Inside, the building was 'some what darke'.

The castle was still habitable a century later and was sketched by Richard

Nunney: from a sketch of 1644

Symonds when he visited in 1644. The owners, the Catholic Prater family, garrisoned it for the king. In September 1645 Colonel Richard Prater and 80 Irish troops, flying a red flag with an obvious Catholic symbol over the steep dormered roof, surrendered after Colonel Rainsborough opened fire under the gaze of Sir Thomas Fairfax. 'A good store of papists' sheltering inside were unharmed but suffered the loss of their property. The castle was slighted, which probably meant little more than internal demolition; the hole made by Rainsborough's cannon was enough.

The building was still in reasonable condition in 1789 when an order was made to make it ready to receive French prisoners, but in the event they probably did not arrive. The roof had long gone by the end of the nineteenth century, and on Christmas Day 1910 the north wall fell. In 1926 Robert Bailey-Neale, lord of the manor, placed it in the guardianship of the then Ministry of Works.

The empty shell reveals something of the internal arrangements: kitchen, stores and the well on the ground floor, servants' quarters on the first. The larger, traceried windows of the second floor clearly indicate the principal rooms with sleeping chambers above. The inscribed altar slab in the chapel in the south-west tower is a reminder of the long Catholic ownership of the building.

Originally there was no terrace at the foot of the walls: the castle emerged, as it were, direct from the moat, and there was a small drawbridge at the entrance. Each tower had a machicolated parapet and there are arrow-slits covering the drawbridge, but neither provide serious defence. To the north-west there are the remains of an embanked bailey but the once surrounding curtain wall has gone.

Source: Leland, *Itinerary*, v. 97; S. E. Rigold, *Guide* (Ministry of Works 1957); M. McGarvie, *Nunney and Trudoxhill* (3rd edn. 1977).

Access: English Heritage; open to public.

Nunney

PORTBURY   ST499753

The so-called 'priory' of Portbury comprises a gutted angle tower and a large angle buttress supporting a building probably of the early sixteenth century and subsequently much restored. The original structure was perhaps a gatehouse giving access to a courtyard around which were a dwelling and agricultural buildings belonging to the grange of the priory of Breamore in Hampshire since the thirteenth century.

Source: E. Green, *Portbury Priory* (1905).

Access: private.

STOKE SUB HAMDON   ST476178

John Beauchamp obtained a licence to crenellate his manor house at Stoke in 1333 and died ten years later. Sir Matthew Gournay seems to have lived there, but owners of the estate after his death in 1406 seem not to have done so and the building then probably fell into decay. In the 1540s Leland wrote of 'very notable ruins of a great manor place or castle', and only the site of the buildings and the garden were known in the 1630s.

In the 1880s it was possible to trace the remains of a gatehouse, dovecot and chapel, and in the 1970s, before the site was developed, part of the perimeter wall and two blocked gateways were visible.

The chapel, the free chapel of St Nicholas, had been founded by 1287. It had more than one altar, and in the early sixteenth century was still an impressive building. Its nave held at least eight tombs, five with recumbent effigies.

Beyond the choir screen were two more tombs, one covered by a memorial brass to Sir Matthew Gournay. Heraldry in stained glass and encaustic tiles presumably illustrated the history of the ownership of the castle. The chapel ceased to be used about 1550.

Source: *V.C.H. Somerset*, iii. 239, 248; *Proc. Som. Arch. Soc.* cxxiv. 61-76.

Access: private houses built on much of the site. The precinct wall may be seen in Castle Street.

SUTTON COURT, Stowey   ST596605

John Leland stayed at the 'old maner place' of Sir John St Loe and described several places in relation to their distance from 'Southetoun'. An earlier Sir John St Loe, either the one who built Newton castle and died in 1314 or his immediate successor, built a tall, square tower with circular stair turret. A hall was built behind the tower in the late fifteenth or earlier sixteenth century, the beginning of the early Tudor transformation of the castle to a country house.

Source: Leland, *Itinerary*, v. 103-4; Pevsner, *North and East Somerset*, 267.

Access: private dwelling.

TORWESTON,   ST091406
Sampford Brett

Adam Brett, descendant of Simon Brito who held half a knight's fee in 1166, as lord of Sampford and Torweston, in 1306 acquired licence for a market and fair at Sampford and for free warren at

Sutton Court, Bishop Sutton: tower and chapel

his home at Torweston. In 1316 Adam, at the instance of Alice de Leygrave, the king's nurse, had licence to crenellate his dwelling at Torweston.

Castle Hill and the field names Back Castle and Castle Coppice, survived in the nineteenth century and a house known as Torweston Barton stood in the garden of the present Torweston farmhouse in the mid eighteenth century.

Source: *V.C.H. Somerset*, v. 173.

Access: private farmland.

WELLS, BISHOP'S PALACE ST552458

In 1207 Bishop Jocelin Trotman received from the Crown a licence to form a park on the south side of the city. This involved, among other things, the diversion of a road from the east end of his garden. From this licence is usually dated the beginning of building work on the Palace, although the presence of an established garden on or near the site suggests that a house already stood nearby.

That earliest work, dated on architectural grounds to the period 1230-50, comprised a two-storey range of first floor hall, solar and gallery over a vaulted undercroft with a garderobe wing at the rear. This range still survives within the central range of the present building. A chapel may have stood on the site of the present one; or rather it is possible that the lower parts of the present chapel are the work of Bishop Jocelin and the higher are a remodelling by Bishop Robert Burnell in the 1280s. It was followed by the great hall which, if by Burnell, must have been before his death in 1292. Opposite the chapel were probably some old kitchens of Jocelin's time and other staff quarters; a new kitchen stood at the far end of the hall. Between these buildings and the cathedral were several houses and two gateways, one of them part of the ceremonial way from the cathedral.

Attacks on people in the bishop's retinue about 1336 led to a radical

Bishop's Palace, Wells, 1825

change in the building after 1340 when Bishop Ralph of Shrewsbury obtain a royal licence to enclose both the cathedral and his own house by walls and to crenellate and make towers and posterns in them. So the bishop's house was surrounded by an irregular pentagon with bastions at each corner and in the middle of the long south side and a gatehouse on the north. Around the whole was a moat fed from St Andrew's well.

Further buildings were added within the walls by Bishop Thomas Bekynton, creating ranges on the two remaining sides of Jocelin's courtyard. Bekynton also built the gatehouse called the Bishop's Eye which was an impressive entrance to the Palace from the Market Place. Only the gatehouse survives from that phase of building, and in the sixteenth century the roof was removed from Burnell's Great Hall. Bishop

Ralph's walls and moat still survive, and visitors often comment on such a charming example of the Church Militant.

Source: R.W. Dunning, 'The Bishop's Palace', in *Wells Cathedral*, ed. L.S. Colchester, 227-44.

Access: open to visitors on limited days.

WEST BOWER, Durleigh   ST266365

The remarkable house now standing on the edge of Durleigh Reservoir was originally part of a courtyard house, the north side of which was dominated by a gatehouse. Only that gatehouse range and the replacement for another range at right angles now survives.

There had been a house at Bower in the early thirteenth century, and soon after Richard Coker bought it in 1335 a

Bishop's Palace, Wells

chapel was licensed there. The gate-house may have been part of a fourteenth-century building, but the polygonal turrets were probably added by Margaret Coker and her husband Sir Alexander Hody, whose initials appear on stained glass in its turret windows. Sir Alexander died in 1461.

Source: *V.C.H. Somerset*, vi. 210-11.

Access: private dwelling.

WOOKEY, Court Farm   ST518458

According to a survey of Wookey manor compiled in 1557, the manor house, leased by Bishop Clerk to his brother Thomas from 1544, was approached from the south-east through a gatehouse which incorporated a porter's lodge and two chambers over. A second entrance through a pair of broad gates and a wicket had another porter's lodge and one room above. Within was a substantial manor house surrounded by yards including one with running water and a fish pond.

The present Court farmhouse incorporates features of the early thirteenth and the fifteenth centuries, the work of bishops Jocelin Trotman and Thomas Bekynton. Both bishops John Stafford (1425-43) and Bekynton (1443-65) used it often. It is assumed that the site was surrounded by a moat, although no such feature was mentioned in 1557, by which time it may have been filled.

Source: Wells Cathedral Library, Chapter Ledger Book D (transcribed

West Bower Manor, Durleigh: gatehouse, 1855

and made available by Miss Joan Hasler).

Access: private dwelling but footpath runs in front of the house.

YARLINGTON   ST654293

A house here in 1208 gave shelter for a night to King John. Simon de Montacute received royal licence to crenellate his house in 1313. By 1484-5 buildings within the moat (*motam cur'*) included a poultry house and a stable, and the whole was let by the lord of the manor to John FitzJames of Redlynch.

The manor house or its successor was demolished about 1782 and was replaced by a new house on a different site. A farmhouse had been built on the site of the former offices and stables by 1723. The remains of the stables were discovered in 1875 and the names Pigeonhouse field and Court field survived for land beside the moat in the early twentieth century.

Sources: *Calendar of Patent Rolls, 1313-17*, 31; P.R.O. SC6/974/6; T. E. Rogers, *Records of Yarlington* (1902), 5-7, 85, 95.

Access: private.

FOLLIES AND FANTASIES

AVISHAYES, Chaffcombe ST354092

On the hill to the east of the house is a small embattled building known as the Castle, built in the nineteenth century. It serves two purposes: an eye-catcher and a water tower.

Source: *V.C.H. Somerset*, iv. 124.

Access: private.

BALLAND'S CASTLE, ST753311
Penselwood

Before 1298 the village and most of the parish of Penselwood lay within Selwood Forest. Although this earthwork has in the past been interpreted as a motte with a bailey, its position makes no military sense. It seems more likely that while the forest was at its greatest extent the mound served as a *tristra* from which hunters could shoot at deer driven past. When the mound ceased to be inside the forest it became the foundation of a lodge for the lieutenant of the forest. The lodge was apparently occupied by Lord Stourton in 1540 and was still standing in 1618. A house bearing the name Forest Lodge was built further north in the eighteenth century.

The name Ballands castle derives from the surrounding fields, formerly woodland, called Ballands. This name, occurring in the fourteenth century in the personal name Baller, probably refers to clay digging on the site.

Source: *Letters and Papers of Henry VIII*, xv, p. 153; S.R.O., DD/WY W/SR 1;

V.C.H. Somerset, draft history of Penselwood.

BANWELL CASTLE, ST403587
Banwell

In the 1950s a painted notice on the door declared: 'Built in the nineteenth century and has no historic or other interest. Kindly remember that this Englishman's Castle is his Home and do not intrude'. The buildings comprise a gatehouse, stable block, walling and dwelling house massively battlemented, turreted and towered, with four-centred archways and subarches in the windows. The whole has been described as 'a good and comprehensive example of a Victorian militaristic conceit'.

The building was erected in the 1840s for a London solicitor, Joseph Dyer Sympson, whose wife was living there in 1851. Robert Trickey, a Banwell builder, worked as a joiner on the entrance doors. Sir George Oatley (d. 1950) restored some of the interiors in a Gothic style.

Source: information from Mr David Bromwich; M.H.L.G. list (1953).

Access: part of the house is open as a catering establishment.

BECKINGTON CASTLE, ST800515
Beckington

This is not a castle but a house which has been given a fanciful history stretching back to 1140 and a pageant of important owners including two of Henry VIII's wives. The builder was

Banwell Castle

probably William Long, a wealthy Wiltshire clothier who died in 1558; and it was the home of the first two earls of Marlborough in the early seventeenth century. Not until 1839 was it called Castle House. All the rest of the nonsense stems from that silly piece of Victorian 'romanticism and pretence'.

Source: M. McGarvie, *The Somerset Magazine*, September 1993, 40-43.

Access: private dwelling.

BURROW MUMP, Lyng   ST359305

The natural hill rising above the Levels where the River Cary used to join the Parrett was an obvious defensive site, but claims that a Norman castle stood there were not proven in excavations published in 1940, and were, in any event, based on a mistaken view that there was a castle on the site in 1315-16. Historically the hill, known during the Middle Ages as la Bereg or Burgh, was a small detached part of Lyng parish, the parish in which Athelney abbey lay, and the connection between the hill and the abbey was made by Collinson. There was a chapel on the hill in the mid thirteenth century.

The obvious strategic importance of the site emerged only when the surrounding Levels had been drained and a bridge built. During the Civil War a fort was built on the hill by the royalists, but was lost by them after the battle of Langport in 1645. Lord Feversham secured the crossing shortly before the battle of Sedgemoor in 1685, perhaps using the earlier defences.

Source: *V. C. H. Somerset*, vi. 55.

Beckington Castle, 1842

Access: Belongs to the National Trust, having been given as a memorial to Somerset men who fell in the First World War.

COMPTON CASTLE,   ST647257
Compton Pauncefoot

The Gothick fantasy designed about 1821 by J. Finden of Bath for John Hubert Hunt seems to incorporate at its western end an earlier house which, from its description in the 1590s, was a medieval or Tudor building approached through a gatehouse. The main house then comprised a hall, parlour, oriel, and two butteries entered from a porch, with seven chambers over, and service rooms probably in a wing behind the butteries including cellar, kitchen, and two larders. Somewhere nearby, possibly forming a rear courtyard, were brewhouse, bulting-house with a chamber above, two barns, two stables, a byre and dovecot, a wood house, a coal house and a two-storyed storehouse. The gatehouse, giving the whole almost the status of a defended house, had rooms above the arched entrance.

Mr Hunt's house is a massive square embattled tower with turreted wings and a central entrance porch. William Phelps, writing in 1836, described the interior entrance hall and staircase as 'highly ornamented in a Gothic style'. The galleried hall is an octagon with a groined ceiling.

The grounds were laid out on an

Burrow Mump

Compton Pauncefoot castle, 1960

extensive scale with a large lake. They were completed only just before Mr Hunt's death in 1830.

Sources: *Recusant Roll 2* (Catholic Record Soc. 1970); Phelps, *History of Somerset*; Colvin, *Biographical Dictionary of British Architects*, 205.

Access: private dwelling.

ENMORE CASTLE, Enmore ST239352

John Perceval, first earl of Egmont (died 1748), spent thousands of pounds to prove to his own satisfaction that he was descended from William, Baron of Yvery, in the early twelfth century. The result was, in modern estimation, 'an impudent fiction'. His son, a rather more genuine antiquarian and anxious to establish himself as a political power near Bridgwater, bought up the estate which had once been the home of the great medieval family of Malet.

The Malets' 'Great House' included a hall and chapel, had 20 hearths in 1664 and was still standing in 1727. It was approached through a gatehouse and would thus have qualified for inclusion here as a fortified house. The house and surrounding land had been acquired by the second earl of Egmont by 1751 and between then and 1755 he designed and built a castle, possibly incorporating the old gatehouse. It was entirely suitable that in 1762 the creator of this fantasy should have been honoured for his political support with an English barony with the splendid medieval title of Lord Lovel and Holland of Enmore.

The building was a hollow square on three floors above a basement, which was surrounded by a moat which was dry but for stew ponds in each corner and stables and store rooms in its outer walls. Access to the moat was by a tunnel entered from some distance away in the park. There were nearly 70 rooms, some in the square and semi-circular turrets.

In 1834 three sides of the building were demolished, and it was further reduced in size and remodelled in the 1930s. Part of the basement and moat still survive.

Source: *V.C.H. Somerset*, vi. 38-9; R. W. Dunning, *Some Somerset Country Houses*, 49-53.

Access: private dwelling.

KNOWLE TOWER, Bawdrip ST333403

An extensive sham castle was built in 1870 for Benjamin Greenhill of Knowle Hall, a Tudor-style house of the 1830s. It was photographed by Robert Gillo when it was newly built and then comprised a completed circular tower, lengths of curtain wall two storeys high, a second, incomplete, tower and some imitation footings of two more towers and walling around an oval courtyard, then laid out as a croquet lawn. The main tower alone was left standing after the Second World War and concern for the safety of the pupils of the school which occupied Knowle Hall led to the decision to demolish in the early 1950s.

Source: *V.C.H. Somerset*, vi. 187; information from the owner, Mrs A.C.N. Hudson, Claverdon, Warwickshire.

Access: private.

Knowle Tower, Bawdrip

MIDFORD CASTLE, Midford

ST759614

Built on a magnificent wooded site above a valley, the house was probably designed by James Wyatt's pupil John Carter for Henry Woolhouse Disney Roebuck, the son of a Newark doctor. A plan for a similar house was published by Carter in 1774 and this was probably built soon afterwards. Its ingenious three-storeyed trefoil plan, three conjoined semi-circles, gave rise more than a century later to the ridiculous story that this 'ace of clubs' plan commemorated a gambling success.

Indeed, only when the porch as added about 1810 for Charles Conolly could the plan even slightly resemble a club. Before then the three-towered building with pretty ogee windows and parapet of pierced quatrefoils, stood on a terrace which was in fact a remarkable substructure which contained domestic offices, coach house and even stables joined by a network of passages and stone vaults. Fine plasterwork inside was probably by Thomas Stocking of Bristol.

There is also a later castellated gatehouse and in the grounds stables, added about 1810, a towered chapel and

Midford Castle

a summer house. A 'hermitage', part of the original concept, seems to have gone by 1788. The chapel was in use until about 1901.

Source: *Country Life*, 3, 10 March 1944.

Access: private dwelling.

SHAM CASTLE,   ST766649
Bathwick Hill, Bath

It is little more than a screen, comprising a central towered arch of three storeys, two-storeyed wings each side and square, two-storeyed end towers. But it was built on Bathwick Hill to provide Ralph Allen with a magnificent eye-catcher from his house in Old Lilliput Alley down in the city. It was probably designed by Sanderson Miller about 1755 and was built seven years later by Richard Jones, clerk of works to Allen.

Source: Pevsner, *North Somerset and Bristol*, 137.

Access: footpath beside golf course.

WALTON CASTLE,   ST416729
Walton in Gordano

About 1615-20 the first Baron Poulett, lord of the manor of Walton, chose the site of an Iron-Age earthwork to build a castellated folly. It comprised an octagonal building with porch and polygonal staircase tower, surrounded by an embattled wall with eight sides joined together by circular towers.
 For long a ruin, and latterly threatened with demolition, it has been converted to a dwelling.

Source: Pevsner, *North Somerset and Bristol*, 274.

Access: private dwelling.

WILLETT TOWER, Elworthy ST096335

Willett Tower, standing on the summit of Willett Hill, was built 'at the expense of the neighbouring gentry' on the Escott estate, no doubt to serve as a 'steeple' for the horsemen of the district. It was finished by 1782.

Source: *V.C.H. Somerset*, v. 69.

Access: private woodland.

Sham Castle, Bath

Walton Castle, Walton in Gordano, 1788

PRISONS

ILCHESTER
ST522227

Castle Farm, on the southern bank of the Yeo just inside the north gate of the town, may have derived its name from the first county gaol there. A building of wood and stone in the 1280s, it came into use in 1166-7, and was regularly repaired by the Crown. It was abandoned in 1280 in favour of a gaol at Somerton. When prisoners were again kept at Ilchester from 1371 it is not certain that they returned to the old gaol. In the sixteenth century they were housed on the bridge, and from 1599 until 1843 on the north side of the river opposite the original site.

Source: *V.C.H. Somerset*, iii. 180, 185.

SOMERTON
ST491286

From 1280 until *c*.1371, when Somerton's gaol was holding county prisoners, the clerks recording the proceedings at assizes regularly referred to the gaol as Somerton castle. The building adjoined a hall of pleas or court house and the churchyard, and a visitor in 1579 recorded 'an old tower embattled about castle-like'. Later antiquarians sought to place the castle in the market place, but that was a medieval house confused with a real castle at Somerton in Lincolnshire.

Source: *V.C.H. Somerset*, iii. 132, 138-9; information from Dr J.B. Post.

BIBLIOGRAPHY

M. Aston and I. Burrow (eds), *The Archaeology of Somerset* (1982)

M. Aston (ed.), *Aspects of the Medieval Landscape of Somerset* (1988)

M. Aston and R. Iles (eds), *The Archaeology of Avon* (1989)

R. Allen Brown, *English Castles* (1970)

J. Collinson, *The History and Antiquities of the County of Somerset* (1791)

D. N. Dumville, *Wessex and England* (1992) [esp. 24-7 on the Burghal Hidage]

R. W. Dunning, 'The Bishop's Palace' in *Wells Cathedral*, ed. L. S. Colchester (1982)

R. W. Dunning, *Some Somerset Country Houses* (1991)

J. E. Jackson, *A Guide to Farleigh Hungerford* (1879)

D. J. Cathcart King, *Castellarium Anglicanum* (2 vols, 1983)

J. Leland, *Itinerary*, ed. L Toulmin Smith (1964)

C. E. Long (ed.), *Richard Symonds' Diary of the Marches of the Royal Army During the Civil War* (Camden Soc, 1859)

H. C. Maxwell-Lyte, *A History of Dunster* (1909)

N. Pevsner, *South and West Somerset* and *North Somerset and Bristol* (1958)

Proceedings of the Somersetshire Archaeological Society

M. W. Thompson, *The Decline of the Castle* (1987)

Victoria History of Somerset, iii-vi, ed R. W. Dunning (1974-92)

W. Worcestre, *Itineraries*, ed. J. Harvey (1969)